C. S. LEWIS AND THE CRISIS OF A CHRISTIAN

GREGORY S. COOTSONA

WESTMINSTER
JOHN KNOX PRESS
LOUISVILLE · KENTUCKY

First edition
Published by Westminster John Knox Press
Louisville, Kentucky

14 15 16 17 18 19 20 21 22 23—10 9 8 7 6 5 4 3 2 1

Book design by Erika Lundbom
Cover design by designpointinc.com

Library of Congress Cataloging-in Publication Data
Cootsona, Gregory S.
   C. S. Lewis and the crisis of a Christian / Gregory S. Cootsona.
      pages cm
   Includes bibliographical references.
   ISBN 978-0-664-23940-4 (paperback)
1. Lewis, C. S. (Clive Staples), 1898-1963. 2. Anglican converts--England--Biography. 3. Christian biography--England. I. Title.
   BV4935.L43C66 2014
   230.092--dc23

2014012362

Most Westminster John Knox Press books are available at special quantity discounts when purchased in bulk by corporations, organizations, and special-interest groups. For more information, please e-mail SpecialSales@wjkbooks.com.

To my parents,
who came to appreciate Lewis later in life than I did
but certainly recognized his genius and creativity nonetheless.

CONTENTS

Chapter 1

INTRODUCING C. S. LEWIS

A young man who wishes to remain a sound Atheist cannot be too careful of his reading. . . . God is, if I may say it, very unscrupulous.

C. S. Lewis, *Surprised by Joy*

I AM WRITING THIS BOOK FOR ONE PRIMARY PURPOSE. THIS IS NOT A biography of C. S. Lewis, a critical denunciation of his theology, nor a piece of hagiography. Instead I am addressing the question of why Lewis remains so popular, selling more books today than when he died in 1963, and why, after decades of reading his work, he still speaks to me. Here's my answer: *Lewis's voice still resonates because his crises and their resolutions in his work reflect our own crises and guide us toward resolution.*

Though not writing a biography, I will begin by telling the story of Lewis's life through the troubles and complexities that shaped him. I will then pursue his thought through his writings—which is what he's best known for—and the way his books, articles, and published addresses offer us access to his wisdom. I approach it this way because Lewis's crises informed his writing, and they give it the power that still resonates today for his readers.

Crises are, as Webster's puts it, "an unstable or crucial time or state of affairs whose outcome will make a difference for better or worse."[1] Whether positive or negative, they always carry with them momentous change. I will describe Lewis's life story line around six main chapters, each (except the first and the last) broadly defining a decade of his sixty-five years. In keeping with the theme of this book, each of these chapters contains critical points when the story of his life altered dramatically, when he confronted these crises and sought to resolve them.

Chapter 1: Lewis was born just before the turn of the twentieth century, on November 29, 1898, in Belfast, Ireland, in a family of four that included his older brother and his best friend, Warren, called "Warnie." His early childhood was happy until his beloved mother, Florence, died of cancer when Lewis was almost ten. Soon after and for the next six years, his father sent him to a series of boarding schools—all of which he detested. Around fourteen, he abandoned his faith. From sixteen to eighteen, Lewis prepared for his university entrance—and more importantly his education was revived—when he moved to Surry and was privately tutored by W. T. Kirkpatrick, or Kirk, whom Lewis named "The Great Knock."

In August of 1908, C. S. Lewis, a nine-year-old boy from Belfast, Ireland, experienced the first major crisis of his life. His beloved mother, Flora, died of cancer. His later reflections reveal the depth of this trauma. By the way, the first thing to do when writing *about* Lewis: read something *he* wrote—something as beautiful, as winsome, as wise, and as touching as what follows.

With my mother's death all *settled happiness*, all that was tranquil and reliable, disappeared from my life. There was to be much fun, many pleasures, many stabs of Joy; but no more of the old security. It was sea and islands now; the great continent had sunk like Atlantis.[2]

Lewis never had a stable, or especially happy, relationship with his father. It was his mother who provided him with tenderness and security. This closing paragraph from the first chapter of his autobiography, *Surprised by Joy*, alludes to both how he later described this tragic moment and how he resolved his crisis. Indeed, this first crisis—the loss of childhood security and its innocence—was deepened as Lewis got sent to boarding schools less than a month after his mother's death. The death of his mother also began gradually to separate him from his father, a relationship that never fully healed. Having knocked out this "settled happiness," he searched to respond and gradually found recourse in cynicism and atheism.

A fight between imagination and reason took hold in Lewis's life. His staunch and rather prickly atheism did not ultimately satisfy him, but he tamped down its voices and found focus and meaning in the dialectics of his beloved teacher Kirkpatrick and the glories of great literature. Consequently, his atheism deepened and became more poignant. Although he was later able to resolve his faith with the suffering of life, that resolution did not happen until after seventeen years of bitterness, cynicism, and depression marked by his potent atheism. "I maintained that God did not exist. I was also very angry with God for not existing."[3] Nonetheless, within this long period of atheism, the seeds of a metamorphosis were sown. At seventeen, he picked up George MacDonald's *Phantastes*, and his imagination, as he phrased it, was "baptized."

In 1917, he began studies in Oxford at University College, but he soon volunteered for military service in WWI, experiencing the horrors of the trenches of the Great War, and he came home wounded in April 1918. Lewis did not write much directly about the war—aside from the stirring sections in *Surprised by Joy* and a few other allusions—but he saw suffering, the depth of which led to a depressive period that wasn't really resolved until his conversion in 1931. The reality of evil in the world—and its companion, pain—worked their way through almost everything he wrote.

Chapter 2: In January 1919, he returned to Oxford, the great city of learning where he would live until his death. During his academic work, he took three exams: Honour Moderations (midway examinations), Greats (classics and philosophy), and English Language and Literature. He received the highest marks, or "firsts," on all three—a feat rarely accomplished. In 1921, as a result of a pact with a fellow soldier, Paddy Moore, that either would support the other's parent if the son died, Lewis moved in with Paddy's mother, Janie Moore, and her daughter, Maureen. He would care for Mrs. Moore until her death in 1951. He began tutoring in 1924 at University College, though his hope was to be a great poet. In 1925, he was elected fellow in English Language and Literature at Magdalen College, Oxford.

Lewis loved the beauty of Oxford as well as its legendary intellectual climate. This was a period of significant intellectual growth and further development of Lewis's rationalism, especially cultivated by the empiricist Logical Positivism and Oxford Realism of the early twentieth century, two philosophies—despite their differences—that argued we can only reasonably talk about what we see and touch. During this time, he also began his life with Janie and Maureen Moore. They moved together to the Kilns outside of Oxford in Headington from June 1921 onward. In fact, even when he was a resident of Magdalen College during those years, the Kilns would be his home for the rest of his life.

So Lewis began his twenties with relative stability, and this stability provided him the opportunity to examine his philosophical convictions. In addition, Lewis desired fame, particularly to be recognized as one of the great poets of the twentieth century. But the tide of poetry was moving away from the metered, rhyming poems that he cherished and wrote. Finally, this brilliant young scholar with three "firsts" could not find a teaching job, and for all his three decades at Oxford, he never moved beyond being a tutor. Consequently, he struggled with financial concerns.

Chapter 3: His father, with whom he had a tumultuous relationship, died in 1929. The next year he became a theist.[4] Then, in 1931, he professed faith in Jesus Christ and became a communicant in the Anglican Church.

Lewis fought against God, especially the idea that God would take away his ability to command and determine his own life. In his room at Magdalen College, every time he lifted his mind from his work, he sensed God's approach. Finally he relented, "admitted that God was God," and became (with pardonable overstatement) "the most dejected and reluctant convert in all England."[5] Becoming a theist, and then a Christian, represents the most significant resolution of crisis in his life. It is the crisis that will fill the following pages more than any other.

Lewis described this famous late-night stroll on the one-mile Addison's Walk outside Magdalen College in Oxford in September 1931, at age thirty-two, in a letter to his childhood friend, Arthur Greeves. After walking with fellow Oxford professors J. R. R. Tolkien and Hugo Dyson, he admitted that his struggle was between pagan "myths"—which, as a lover of classical literature, he cherished—and the uniqueness of the story of Jesus and his discovery that "Christ is simply a true myth." Interestingly, his first adult Christian communion on Christmas Day 1931 occurred at about the mathematical midpoint of his life.

The way he resolved the crisis of his unbelief first, and then of believing in Jesus Christ as the Son of God secondly, echoes through his apologetics and really through all his writing. His argument against naturalism (a belief that the world of nature is all there is), the argument from desire (or joy) for natural law as it points to the lawgiver, and their fulfillment in Jesus Christ as Lord, as well as his conviction that Christianity doesn't invalidate, but instead fulfills, the best of paganism—all derive from this intellectual breakthrough. It also allowed him to combine his great imagination with his searching reason in a potent blend.

Chapter 4: His first major breakthrough in religious writing came after his broadcast talks for the BBC—first recorded in 1941 and later published in 1952 as *Mere Christianity*. This began a periodic of significant literary output. It also presented a new crisis: the crisis of fame.

For readers who cherish—or perhaps even idolize—Lewis's specifically Christian writings, the 1940s were the period of great flowering; here, for example, one finds *The Screwtape Letters, Mere Christianity,* and *Miracles.* It is for me, and for those I've talked with, a time when a treasure trove of Christian insight was unleashed. Nonetheless, there are at least two attendant crises in his later fame. For Lewis, fame represented a kind of crisis—becoming a spokesperson. It was a task, according to the *Time* article that accompanied his front-cover picture, that he found a chore and blamed on the unscrupulousness of God. For example, when Lewis's picture appeared on the September 8, 1947, cover of *Time* magazine, the heading read "Oxford's C.S. Lewis, His Heresy: Christianity." In the article, Lewis said, "I certainly never intended being a hot gospeler. If I had only known this when I became a Christian!"[6]

But Lewis wasn't just a spokesperson, he was a popularizer, or better yet, a *translator*: "People praise me for being a translator. But where are the others? I wanted to start a school of translation."[7] Without others alongside, and seeing this critical need, he took up the task of translation and became the best-known Christian apologist of the twentieth century. And with it came a sea of letters—to which he dutifully responded daily—as well as jealousy and resistance among his intellectual and unbelieving colleagues at Oxford.

Chapter 5: After losing a debate in 1948 at the Oxford Socratic Club with the famous philosopher and Catholic Elizabeth Anscombe, Lewis moved from apologetics proper and into fiction. He began publishing his famous series The Chronicles of Narnia in 1950, which continued until 1956. Mrs. Moore died in 1951. The next year, he met Joy Gresham in person for the first time. Having been voted down for a professorship at Oxford, Cambridge subsequently offered him a chaired professorship in Medieval and Renaissance Literature, and he started teaching there in January 1955. That same year he received the greatest honor for any scholar in the humanities: election to the British Academy.

This period marked a transition to another kind of religious writing. He also confessed in a letter from 1950 that his well of creativity was dry, and he had submitted his craft to whatever God designed. His muse soon returned, and he moved into a period of focusing on fantasy writing and began to write The Chronicles of Narnia. Many—notably A. N. Wilson in his vivid, yet somewhat snarky, biography of Lewis[8]—have argued that Lewis's defeat in the debate with Elizabeth Anscombe occasioned his retreat from apologetics. But it seems more clear—as I'll develop below—that through this crisis, Lewis realized the weakness of direct apologetics. Instead he sought to show rather than tell his readers why they ought to take Christian faith seriously and joyfully. The debate with Anscombe, though difficult, represented not simply a defeat but a recognition for Lewis. He realized he had not kept up with the currents in academic philosophy.

Another major transition was the death of Mrs. Moore. Although Lewis cared deeply for her, her passing was also a relief and allowed him more time to read books and write. Though he was disappointed that he did not receive a professorship at Oxford, receiving one at Cambridge freed him from his tutoring duties, giving him more time. He also found Cambridge more congenial to his faith. These two critical changes opened a new space for his imagination.

Finally, during his fifties, he met Joy, sixteen years his junior, a divorcée from New York City with two young boys.

Chapter 6: He married Joy Davidman, an American divorcée with two young sons, in 1956. She died on July 13, 1960. In response, he wrote *A Grief Observed.* After a brief, serious illness—including a coma the preceding summer—he died on November 22, 1963.

I'll have more to say about the details in the pages that follow, but this final chapter of Lewis's life initiates both great delight and profound sorrow for Lewis. Marrying this brilliant writer from New York City, he ultimately discovered an intellectual and romantic companion. He respected Joy's mind, and for her part, she devoured and cherished his writings. And yet, when he learned of Joy's illness, Lewis faced a familiar crisis: a mother dying of cancer with two young sons. He probably even saw his own early life being replayed. Despite prayers for recovery and a subsequent brief reprieve, Joy succumbed to bone cancer after a few brief, but happy, years of marriage.

Lewis was crushed, although it did not destroy his rational faith, as many have argued. It helped him to draw a full circle back to his first apologetic work, *The Problem of Pain*. Most significantly, Lewis's own death gives special poignancy to his reflections on afterlife. He did not begin with a robust faith in a life to come, but he realized this was the only way to resolve the crisis of death—that our life on this earth comes to an end and presents a great question about the goodness of God.

THE PROMISE OF CRISIS

The road I'm treading, "Lewis through crisis," represents the difficulties and complexities Lewis faced and their resolutions. But I am also writing about interlocking crises and their resolutions. This book addresses the crisis of my own life that found satisfying responses (and keeps discovering more) in Lewis's writings, and I've seen that satisfaction mirrored in readers of Lewis's works whom I've met, read, or pastored over the past two decades. They have also found resolution of their crises in Lewis's work.

Because I'm talking about *readers* of C. S. Lewis (and not, for example, those students or friends who knew him in life), I have focused my research for this book on reading what Lewis wrote. I have concentrated on rereading his corpus. When I have done research at the two libraries that house Lewis's papers—Wheaton College's Wade Collection, housed in the beautiful suburbs of Chicago, and the materials at Oxford University's glorious Bodleian Library—I have focused on Lewis's manuscripts and personal library to see how *he* wrote. I have learned a great deal from the biographies of Lewis—from the one written by George Sayer, Lewis's former student and later close friend, which offers an intimate and sympathetic yet realistic rendering of Lewis;[9] from Wilson's exquisitely written, compelling, and generally more critical portrait;[10] and most recently from Alister McGrath's meticulous, unparalleled but somewhat drab work on the fiftieth anniversary of Lewis's death.[11] But these I've studied as secondary sources, focusing on what I've learned through reading Lewis's books. All research for this book focused on reading Lewis rather than reading *about* Lewis.

So I am addressing how C. S. Lewis tackled his crises. For the discerning Lewis reader, I need to defend myself briefly against what Lewis called "the Personal Heresy"—the idea that a book or idea derives solely from an author's biography and therefore discusses not the work, but the author.[12] Though it was fashionable when Lewis practiced literary criticism, he detested this approach and countered that, in reading criticism of poetry, we need to learn more about the *poem*, not the personality of the poet. I take much of what he argued to be accurate, particularly in how it focuses us as readers to attend to the words authors actually write. We attend to what is on the page, not behind it. If I need, nonetheless, to defend my searching out the crises that formed Lewis's writing, my response is this: first of all, I am not writing primarily about Lewis's fiction. Fiction is designed to work primarily as a story; nonfiction invites personal engagement and questions about *why* the writer is interested in the topic at hand.

Secondly and most importantly, Lewis was fundamentally a practical, not speculative, thinker. So he forged his insights from his experience. Put simply, I'm not trying to discern Lewis's personality through his writings but to discern his philosophy of life. As Sayer writes, "He never merely thought ideas; he also felt them. . . . It was consistent with Jack's character, given his practicality and sense of purpose, that philosophy did not remain for him a purely speculative occupation."[13] Or as Lewis himself recounted in *Surprised by Joy*, in a conversation with Dom Bede Griffiths and Owen Barfield where Lewis referred to philosophy as a "subject," he received this response: "'It wasn't a *subject* to Plato,' said Barfield, 'it was a way.'" Lewis then commented that Griffiths's agreement and a glance between the two exposed his "frivolity."[14]

He knew something had to change. For that reason, he was glad to have left the "bleak and questioning" atmosphere of pure philosophy when he decided to take up the study of literature.[15] There is a point at which enough speculation has taken place, Lewis concluded, and something needed to be done—his philosophy (and later theology) needed to become practical and therefore practiced. This insight into Lewis's mind will recur as an important theme throughout this book. For this reason, Lewis brought his own crises to his writing.

And why read Lewis's crises through his *writing*? Here I take in what his stepson Douglas Gresham records about Lewis's response to the death of his wife, Joy, in July 1960:

> He did what he always did under extreme stress. He sat down at his desk, and looking into himself and carefully observing what was happening deep in his mind where we keep our inmost secrets, he picked up his pen and an old exercise book and began to write.[16]

Lewis worked out his most complex problems—here a particularly poignant and painful one—through his writings. Most of us would simply cry, engage in self-pity, or mope. But Lewis resolved his crises through his scratchy, nibbed pen. In fact, to read his voluminous correspondence—now collected in more than 5,000 pages—is to comprehend that he wanted to relieve others' doubts, spiritual confusion, and despair. And we are the better for all Lewis offers us in our crises.

My conviction is that crises generally open us up to new insights and free us from previously held patterns. The resolutions we seek are, as a rule, much deeper than when we "are at ease in Zion" (to use one of Lewis's favorite phrases, found in Amos 6:1). Thus, to look at Lewis in crisis demonstrates the

depth of his work. In these critical moments, we are exception-
ally open to new insights. Lewis had them, and I will describe
the way these moments transformed readers throughout this
book. Crises have past, present, and future implications: we
take what has come before, all our personal preparation of
character; we experience the crisis; and then we define our
future. In these crises, the person or idea that mediates our
discoveries is key because that helps define the "new normal"
after the crisis transformation is over. We will explore ways
Lewis is a trustworthy mediator and mentor.

I have become convinced that most readers of Lewis are
drawn to his writing because they find resolution to their crises in his work. One particular example is found in my own
blog, where I have posted on Lewis for the past few years as
I've done research for this book. The most popular post, which
dwarfs all others by about twenty to one, is "C. S. Lewis and
the Crisis of Suffering." (I return to that topic in chapter 8.)
It's clear: people want Lewis to help them make it through
places of pain. And pain initiates crises.

To be sure, the issues in Lewis's work, particularly his theological breakthroughs, are not just personal. He spoke Chris-
tianly in a Western culture he clearly saw moving toward being
"post-Christendom" (as he made clear in his opening lecture
at Cambridge[17]), if indeed that state hadn't already arrived.
Honestly, when this fact struck me as I was heading toward
the final drafts of this book, I found myself saying, "It's amazing C. S. Lewis ever became so popular." It's not amazing that
Dante or Milton were well regarded in their day, but Lewis in
post-Christian England? That makes his accomplishments—
of speaking about Christian faith to an increasingly secular
world—that much more impressive.

I think that's why Lewis might be even more relevant today
to the United States. In some similar ways, American society,
which has lagged behind Europe in its de-christening, is also in

a spiritual crisis, and for this reason his resolution of crises in a post-Christian society resonates for us in the United States. I write this book at a time when atheism and those who profess no religious identity (or the "Nones") have only become stronger. Lewis's ideas are again finding themselves put to the test. By some counts, 30 percent of our country now professes no religious belief or an outright belief in atheism.[18] So that leads to several pointed questions, and Lewis, who clearly thought of himself as living in a "post-Christian" Europe, posed these questions himself. Is belief in God legitimate? Is belief in God rational? Is belief in God something worthy of our attention? I will look at the way Lewis presents Christian faith while taking modern context into account; we live in a time when books by the New Atheists, such as Richard Dawkins, Christopher Hitchens, and Daniel Dennett, fill the bookshelves.

Certainly, Lewis did not take on the New Atheists, but the older, mid-twentieth-century ones, especially their use of science as a bludgeon against Christian faith. Questions about whether science invalidates belief and whether the increase in natural knowledge has edged out supernatural occurrences such as miracles—these concerns fill the papers he presented during the 1940s at the Oxford Socratic Club, which openly debated the truth of Christianity.[19] Lewis believed that "the Scientific Outlook," as he named it in one of these papers (that science defines all truth),[20] needed to be countered by good argument. I will return to that topic in chapter 2.

ST. CLIVE IN MY CRISIS

Admittedly, some are offended by the clear Christian elements in Lewis's books, perhaps concluding that he hadn't fully resolved crises for them. As I strolled through a bookshop in the hipster beach town of Santa Cruz a few years ago, I browsed some staff recommendations, including one for *Till*

We Have Faces. It suggested that if readers liked the Narnia books but found their Christian allegory a bit too obvious, they might enjoy this retelling of the Cupid and Psyche story from the viewpoint of the "ugly" older sister. *Till We Have Faces,* the recommendation said, offers a poignant meditation on changing our minds, even about everything we think we know.

Others have argued that Lewis made the resolution of crises too easy, so we can't trust his resolutions. I remember when I was at Berkeley studying medieval literature, I told another student I wanted to read Lewis. He opined (and I paraphrase), "Be careful—his analogies are very crafty and deceptive." I think he was offering a warning about Lewis's apologetics, and apparently his feeling was that Lewis resolved crises too quickly . . . and even maliciously. But his concerns seemed overwrought since I was just reading Lewis's scholarly treatment of courtly love poetry, *The Allegory of Love*!

More importantly, by that time I didn't need his warning: I had already accepted Christianity as a freshman in college. I entered Cal as a functional atheist, but I began to have a crisis about my doubting God. Clive Staples Lewis—or as I jokingly call him today, "St. Clive"—accompanied me on this journey and eventually led me to finding God.

How did he do that? For one thing, I rarely found Lewis simplistic or pat. In fact, in him I found a kindred spirit—one for whom faith was by no means self-evident or devoid of serious reflection, a person who struggled with Jesus as a unique revelation of God, who took religious faith seriously with all his powers of thought. I found in his writings a fluidity of style and of mind that slowly engaged and even entranced me as a fellow lover of books and a soon-to-be undergraduate in comparative literature. And I also found in him a fellow seeker who spent his life in a secular, world-class university, a place where Christianity, if treated at all, was passé, a vestige of Western civilization that had long ago thrown off such infantile beliefs.

It was sometime in the last year or two of high school that I had read *Mere Christianity*, Lewis's presentation and defense of Christianity (two tasks that almost always appeared together for him no matter what the subject). Frivolity—the sort that's commonly called "senioritis"—led me to set Lewis aside for a year. So when I returned to *Mere Christianity* in college, I was astonished: here a writer, a *Christian* at that, was somehow making the whole Christian faith reasonable. I mean, I had been taught that Christianity was anything but reasoned. The most reasonable author I had read to date was also a proponent of this severely unreasoned faith. Lewis taught me that Christian faith requires and sustains serious reflection, but it is not ultimately somber. The content of faith is important, serious but never frivolous: "Christianity, if false, is of *no* importance, and if true, of infinite importance. The only thing it cannot be is moderately important."[21] In fact, faith and the experience of God lead to joy. In this way, Lewis both presented, and later resolved, a crisis.

And although I didn't fully know who this Lewis guy was, nor what a truly world-class mind he possessed, he *made sense.* It was so similar to a sentiment that Lewis himself would record—and which I read many years later—about his own reading, as a young atheist, of the Catholic journalist G. K. Chesterton and his book *The Everlasting Man* that set out "the whole Christian outline of history" in a quite reasonable form, concluding that he was "the most sensible man alive 'apart from his Christianity.' Now, I veritably believe, I thought—I didn't of course *say;* words would have revealed the nonsense—that Christianity itself was very sensible 'apart from its Christianity.'"[22]

Even in this citation, Lewis demonstrates that, though witty (i.e., the irony of attempting to believe Christianity is sensible "apart from its Christianity"), he was never frivolous. As his friends would remind us, Lewis was a very *funny* man.

As his former student Alastair Fowler once remarked, "Lewis seemed always on the verge of hilarity—between a chuckle and a roar."[23] But he knew that humor could also lead to trivializing important topics. In his famous, imagined correspondence between a senior and a junior devil about how to tempt the human soul, *The Screwtape Letters,* he called it Flippancy when the joke is always assumed. "No one actually makes it; but every serious subject is discussed in a manner which implies that they have already found a ridiculous side to it."[24] Accordingly, his humor supported his exposition but never dominated or diminished it.

Lewis taught me that Christian faith could withstand serious intellectual engagement. And Lewis engaged instead of simply defending in his apologetics. In fact, as I interrogated other philosophers—the thought of French poststructuralist Michel Foucault was hot at Berkeley in those days—they actually didn't stand up as well. And so I was being won over, and I began to engage it. Or better, through Lewis's writings, God began to engage me. "I read in a periodical the other day that the fundamental thing is how we think of God. By God Himself it is not! How God thinks of us is not only more important, but infinitely more important."[25] And God, I was learning, apparently thought enough of me to send Christ and to take my questions seriously. I was taken so seriously that I was being shaken—shaken so that I could then be stabilized. My crisis of doubt found an answer in the gospel, and I can attribute a fair measure of this to Lewis.

This leads me back to my reason for writing this book: Even though Lewis has been dead for more than half a century and lived in a world quite different from ours, I believe he can do this—resolve the crises we have with unbelief, belief, and simple human travails—for this generation.

AN OUTLINE OF THIS BOOK

When I finally made my way—by a long and winding road—into the Christian church as a pastor, I found that I gradually leaned more and more on "St. Clive" to describe what this life of faith looks like or ought to resemble. His words and his thoughts have accompanied me into the pulpit, given me inspiration in adult education classes, and wound their way into moments where I needed to offer comfort to those grieving and particular insights about belief in an increasingly unbelieving world.

I offer a brief outline of the key sections of this book. I organized these sections around Lewis's own engagement with these topics: first of all, three chapters on the crises particular to atheism that describe why atheism proved ultimately unsatisfying for Lewis; then two chapters on the crises specific to the Christian faith; and finally, three chapters on crises that no human being—whether believer or not—can escape, even if Lewis learned to resolve these crises through his faith.

The Crises of Atheism

Lewis was a profound thinker who grappled with significant intellectual issues. He struggled with his own doubt about God and whether his atheism could withstand scrutiny. For that reason, his apologetics have helped many and can be grouped as follows: the crisis of materialism, the argument with the most contemporary resonance that naturalism is self-defeating; the crisis of meaninglessness, his case that we sense there is something more than the things of this world; and finally, the crisis of anomie, the argument that natural law implies God as the lawgiver.

The Crises of Christian Faith

Lewis also wrestled with two significant topics particular to Christian belief. First of all, the crisis of other myths: How do I believe in the uniqueness of Christ when there are so many religions? Lewis took this question on more personally in his letters, but it is also featured in his most famous argument—found in *Mere Christianity* and presented in other short articles such as "What Are We to Make of Jesus Christ?"— that Jesus is liar, Lord, or lunatic. Secondly, the crisis of the Bible: How can the Bible have unique authority among all other books?

The Crises of Human Life

Finally Lewis worked hard with three issues that no human being can escape. The crisis of feeling: What do I do when "it doesn't feel right"? This is a problem that plagues Americans who have become convinced to believe the dictum that "if it feels right, do it," and thus when it doesn't feel right, something must be wrong. The crisis of suffering: How are we to live in a world of pain, and is there any purpose to suffering? The crisis of death, which offers a fitting end to our study of Lewis as we face the ultimate and final crisis: What do I do when I stand before my own death? Lewis pointed to the God who gives us hope for our true destiny: a life with the God who created us.

FRANCIS COLLINS AND THE RESOLUTION OF CRISIS

Through these reflections on Lewis, I'll weave narratives of those who have read Lewis and found resolution for their own crises (some of whom I've cared for and known as their pastors). These stories are to come, but I will also close this introduction with one such encounter.

Lewis's writings resolved a critical spiritual and intellectual crisis for the famous geneticist and head of the National Institutes of Health, Francis Collins, perhaps the most prominent scientist in the United States. In his important bestselling work, *The Language of God*, which seeks to reconcile Christian faith with contemporary evolutionary genetics, Collins recounts his experience of reading Lewis as a seeker in medical school. A patient whose faith supported her through terrible heart pain asked him, "What about you? What do you believe?" He could only mutter, "Well, I don't think I believe in anything." He realized that he had never looked at the evidence for or against God and found this a "thoroughly terrifying experience." Upon request, a Methodist pastor handed him a key apologetics text.

> The book was *Mere Christianity* by C. S. Lewis. In the next few days, as I turned its pages, struggling to absorb the breadth and depth of the intellectual arguments laid down by this legendary Oxford scholar, I realized that all of my constructs against the plausibility of faith were those of a schoolboy. Clearly I would need to start with a clean slate to consider this most important of all human questions. Lewis seemed to know all of my objections, sometimes even before I had quite formulated them. He invariably addressed them within a page or two.[26]

Collins represents exactly the kind of person Lewis so often becomes associated with—a seeker honestly looking for God in moments of deep personal crisis. Lewis did speak, and continues to communicate powerfully, to these seekers at critical times. He can do the same today.

The Crises of Atheism

Chapter 2

THE CRISIS OF MATERIALISM

The key to my books is Donne's maxim, "The heresies that men leave are hated most." The things I assert most vigorously are those I resisted long and accepted late.

C. S. Lewis, *Surprised by Joy*

CLIVE STAPLES LEWIS REPRESENTS, BY MANY ACCOUNTS, THE MOST effective apologist in the twentieth century. In beginning this section by describing Lewis as an *apologist*, I will start with a common definition: "someone who makes a reasoned defense of the Christian faith." This definition derives from the Greek word *apologia*, which signified a defense in a court of law. The Greek word *apologia* appears in the New Testament in 1 Peter 3:15. (Incidentally, throughout the book biblical citations are from the King James Version because that is the translation Lewis knew best and used most frequently.) It reads, "Be ready always to give an answer to every man that asketh you a reason of the hope that is in you. . . ."

To be sure, Lewis didn't start out as an effective apologist. His first published attempt at a Christian apologetics, *The Pilgrim's Regress*, was written in a hasty fortnight and does not represent an unmitigated success. It is overly dense, heavy-handed in its criticism of his opponents, and both overly obvious and unnecessarily obscure with characters like Marxomanni, Mussolimini, and Swastici. Though we can sympathize with the profound passion contained in this allegory, Lewis lacked, in this early attempt, the light touch that characterized the majority of his published work.

But Lewis *became* a great apologist because of his emerging winsome style and what he embodied. In a simple sense, this brilliant scholar and fluid writer, known for his faith and not associated with any party or denomination, would become an engaging exponent of "mere Christianity." Clive Staples Lewis, don at Magdalen College, Oxford, represented exactly the type of apologist that Ashley Simpson needed for his "Christian Challenge" series in the early 1930s—Lewis's contribution was *The Problem of Pain*—and that the BBC wanted for their broadcast talks in 1941.

But why did Lewis say yes to these offers and keep producing apologetics? Why not simply stay in the fields of the academy instead of trying to write for a broader audience? I once asked well-known commentator on Lewis and founding member of the New York C. S. Lewis Society, Jim Como, why Lewis did this work—why this brilliant academic didn't just stay in the safe cocoon of Oxford University. He replied quite simply (and I paraphrase): "Because no one else was doing it, and Lewis saw it as his Christian duty." Lewis stated this quite simply in his introduction to *Mere Christianity:* "Ever since I became a Christian I have thought that the best, perhaps the only, service I could do for my unbelieving neighbors was to explain and defend the belief that has been common to nearly all Christians at all times."[1] This question hung around in my mind, and as I reflected further on this puzzle, I discerned another reason: *Lewis simply believed that Christianity was true, and he was convinced that truth was worth arguing for.* And at those moments of contending for the truth, the voice of his father, Albert, the Ulster lawyer, emerged in his son. "Jack" (as he was called by close friends) loved argument and delighted in victory—whether at the Oxford Socratic Club or with close friends such as J. R. R. Tolkien and Own Barfield, who were members of a society of writers and thinkers known as the Inklings—they often met twice weekly to read their work and debate. Lewis cared so much about truth that he was convinced others needed to be convinced, so he became an apologist.

My theme is crises, and apologetics seeks to resolve them. Seekers might say, "I can't believe although I want to—my head isn't convinced." Lewis helps here. Indeed, as Anthony Burgess states, on the cover of my cherished paperback Mac-Millan editions of Lewis's key apologetics, "Lewis is the ideal persuader for the half-convinced, for the man who would like to be a Christian but finds his intellect getting in the way." He spoke rationally and with conviction. So he helps the half-converted. But he also helps resolve the crisis of atheism. By his early thirties, atheism had begun to run out of steam for Lewis. So he had to figure out how to resolve things intellectually.

Not only seeking to persuade others, apologists are often on a quest to convince themselves, and Lewis is an impressive example. Because of his sojourn with atheism from age fourteen to thirty-one, resolving the crisis of unbelief presented considerable task. As the quote at the epigraph of this chapter indicated, Lewis worked particularly hard at heresies he once held to. Put simply, Lewis had to continue to convince himself (as all converts do) that Christianity is true. As a convert myself, this is perhaps the most compelling aspect of his writing. But not the only one. Millions of believers—whether converts or not—also appreciate his work. Not too long ago, Lewis was dubbed by *Time* magazine the "hottest theologian" of the year.[2] And this reminds me of a conversation with an editor of a prominent book company who quipped, "Of course Lewis is popular. He makes it easy for conservative Christians. He does their thinking for them." Though I can't fully disagree, the truth is also not quite that simple. Lewis's writings always engage our thinking as readers. Debra Winger studied Lewis in preparation for her role as Lewis's wife, Joy Davidman, in the film *Shadowlands* and offered this evaluation of Lewis: "He may make difficult *questions* accessible. I don't think he makes answers 'easy.' I don't think he answers questions. He discusses them."[3]

And as Lewis discussed the questions of Christian truth, he gradually constructed a substantial edifice for theological defenses of faith.

LEWIS'S FOUR-PART APOLOGETIC STRATEGY

There are several major and minor apologetic arguments that Lewis produced. For example, in chapter 8, I will focus on his defense of God's goodness and power in the face of suffering. With that in mind, in the next four chapters I will focus on the same number of arguments. These in fact form an interlocking four-part apologetic strategy, which Lewis worked out in the golden age of his apologetic work in the 1940s. Each argument builds on the conclusions of the previous argument. Here is an overview:

1. First of all, in order to even begin steps toward belief, we have to see that there is more to the world than just material stuff. Lewis argues that naturalism or materialism, which is the idea that there is just brute matter, is self-defeating because rational thinking is impossible if we are pure materialists. *Miracles* centrally presents this apologetic, but it is scattered throughout his writings, especially in those he presented at the Oxford Socratic Society in the '40s such as "Is Theology Poetry?" (This also presents the corollary: we cannot discount the miraculous on a priori grounds that it is impossible,

which is the wider concern of *Miracles*. For reasons of space, I will not unfold this entire apologetic here. Moreover, Lewis's argument against materialism has proven to be the most enduring feature of this strategy.)

2. Having established that there is more than nature, Lewis proceeded to something more personal or existential— by which I mean ideas that relate to our existence. Human beings seek something that this world cannot satisfy, which points to a God beyond this world. This argument appears first in *The Pilgrim's Regress*, later in *The Problem of Pain*, and most definitively in his sermon "The Weight of Glory" and throughout *Surprised by Joy*. Lewis established what he called the numinous and later identified with his own quest for joy.

3. Having determined that there is something more, Lewis moved toward the argument that, like the laws of nature, there exists a law or rule about right and wrong (or the law of nature). It is perceived in the conscience of all human beings and points to the God who created that law within us. Lewis developed this apologetic in his opening broadcast talk for the BBC, which became the first section of *Mere Christianity*, as well as in his 1943 Riddell Lectures at the University of Durham that were published as *The Abolition of Man*. This is a crucial move because it establishes a particular character to which our sense of joy points us. Or put another way, joy and beauty are tied to morality.

4. Finally, his argument becomes specifically Christian: Jesus Christ is the fulfillment not only of human myths but also of our human quest for joy and moral truth. Lewis argues that Jesus must be one of three options: liar, Lord, or lunatic. Lewis concludes that the only reasonable answer is that he is Lord. This argument appears principally in *Mere Christianity*.

Each of these arguments responds in some way to crises Lewis had to work through—in fact, attacks he once made against Christian belief—and thus ones that his readers have experienced. These arguments can be separated, and I will unfold each with some care, paying particular attention to the crises that Lewis resolved through each argument.

But these four also interrelate. In one sense, then, Lewis provided four main masterful defenses of Christianity. This makes him an apologist. But there is more to the history of apologetics as a discipline, and certainly this characterization of apologist is inadequate for how Lewis practiced the craft. Here I add the more subtle definition presented by Earl Palmer, the pastor of First Presbyterian Church of Berkeley, whose love for Lewis kindled mine and who described Lewis in a lecture at the church in 1985 as "someone who presents the Christian faith fully aware of the arguments that are presented against it."[4] Palmer also added that an apologist must have *two fluencies: a fluency in the Gospel*, knowing what's central and what's peripheral, and *a fluency in culture*, knowing the cultural norms and language into which this message is presented. Lewis was masterful at both, and I think Palmer's description helps us see that Lewis was always seeking to persuade even when he was simply presenting the Christian faith. Perhaps he was always trying to root out the atheism that still clung to him from his teens and twenties. This double fluency made Lewis a master apologist who resolved the crises of atheism for many readers and was thereby dubbed by Chad Walsh as "apostle to the skeptics."[5]

So Lewis was a brilliant, motivated, and gifted apologist, and I will set his apologetics within the context of the ways he sought to resolve his own crises of atheism. For that reason, it's now time to consider Lewis's next resolution of the internal crisis of atheism: his argument that naturalism is self-defeating. Put simply, Lewis tells us not to be stuck in this world because that position is self-defeating. This argument seems remarkably contemporary in light of the New Atheists, who impugn any notion of something immaterial, of the soul, and therefore of God.

THE PROBLEM OF NATURALISM

Naturalism (and the nearly synonymous position of materialism) represents the philosophical position that the natural world (or the material world in the case of materialism) is all there is, without remainder. At one point in his key argument against naturalism, *Miracles: A Preliminary Study*, Lewis states his definition succinctly, "Some people believe that nothing exists except Nature. I call these people *Naturalists*."[6] In accord with Lewis, I will generally use the term "naturalism" because that is Lewis's preferred term, but sometimes I will employ "materialism" interchangeably. This philosophical position obviously presents problems for Christian faith, which points to God as the Source of all being beyond this material world. In this chapter, I will look at Lewis's apologetic strategy of arguing that naturalism is self-defeating.

Whatever it is called, naturalism has again returned with renewed vigor, though not always with improved insight. And with it a combative anti-theism has arisen in our country. The prominent Harvard neuroscientist Steven Pinker has laid down the gauntlet in this way:

> The neuroscientific worldview—the idea that the mind is what the brain does—has kicked away one of the intuitive supports of religion. So even if you accepted all of the previous scientific challenges to religion—the Earth revolving around the sun, animals evolving, and so on—the immaterial soul was always one last thing that you could keep as being in the province of religion. With the advance of neuroscience, that idea has been challenged.[7]

It seems that materialism has won the day with scientists and that, according to many, it represents the crucial contemporary argument against religious faith. It also represents a crucial component of the New Atheism of Hitchens, Pinker, Dawkins, and Dennett.

In the conflict between Christian faith and naturalism, Lewis's next apologetic argument, even if he formulated it most definitively almost seventy years ago, still takes hold. We have a contemporary culture that hears the siren cries of naturalism. Lewis's argument that naturalism is self-defeating is powerful, and its force cannot be escaped.

OXFORD IN THE 1940S

To understand the context for this strategy, we have to grasp the philosophical setting: Oxford University in the 1940s. Though it can be argued that idealism still maintained a foothold, Lewis nevertheless felt compelled to engage in dialectics against naturalism.[8] For Lewis the big crises with naturalism first emerged in 1930, when he became a theist, and then in 1931, when he looked specifically to Christ. No longer content simply to remain the rationalist—and thus materialist—he found that life had more to offer. In some ways, it could be argued that Lewis had a strong line of idealism running through his philosophical veins, at least in the sense described by his friend, the Oxford philosophical theologian Austin Farrer:

> Lewis was raised in the tradition of an idealist philosophy which hoped to establish the reality of the mental subject independently of, or anyhow in priority to, that of the bodily world.[9]

Farrer does note that Lewis "moved some way from such positions," primarily by concluding that idealism did not sufficiently take in the personal presence of the absolute in the

Incarnation. He indeed calls this shift a move from "ideal-ism," by which he means that there is a transcendent Mind or Spirit, to full encounter with God. This God could never be contained solely by the interactions of the natural world.

There was sufficient idealism in Lewis's convictions to butt heads with the more materialist currents of his day. For example, in Oxford's Socratic Society—where Lewis presented the two pieces (or at least parts thereof) that I am analyzing—Lewis found he regularly had to impugn the arguments of logical positivists, who asserted that statements about a transcendent reality were meaningless. This represents a linguistic and philosophical complement to naturalism. As he wrote to his student Dom Bede Griffiths on April 22, 1954,

> Don't imagine that the Logical Positivist menace is over. To me it seems that the apologetic position has never in my life been worse than it is now. At the Socratic the enemy often wipe the floor with us. *Quousque domine?* [How long, O Lord?][10]

Lewis gloried in moving against the grain of the culture—promoting the role as a "dinosaur" in his opening lecture at Cambridge in 1954.[11] Therefore, it did not bother him to argue for the irrationality of materialism. I use "irrationality" advisedly because Lewis argued that materialism did not allow for rationality and thus obviated truth as well. In materialism, things just *are*; they are neither true nor false. And I mean this literally—Lewis concluded that, if we take nature to be all that there is, there is no place for rational thought. That is why naturalism defeats itself. It cuts off the very branch on which it sits.

As I mentioned above, we live in an age remarkably similar to Lewis's . . . at least in this regard. The intellectual culture of the 1940s endorsed the concept that matter was all that mattered, and Lewis's two prominent writings, "Is Theology

Poetry?" and then *Miracles: A Preliminary Study*, emerged from this culture. For this reason, these two pieces are still pertinent.

Certainly not all scientists today or in the early decades of the twentieth century were of similar minds. Some, even within the naturalist and therefore atheistic camp, saw the problems inherent in simply arguing that "the mind is what the brain does." Lewis quotes the famous geneticist, evolutionary biologist, and atheist John Burdon Sanderson Haldane in *Miracles*:

> It seems to me immensely unlikely that mind is a mere by-product of matter. For if my mental processes are determined wholly by the motions of atoms in my brain I have no reason to suppose that my beliefs are true... and hence I have no reason for supposing my brain to be composed of atoms.[12]

It is noteworthy that Lewis takes up this citation directly in *Miracles*, probably to demonstrate that the self-defeating nature of unremitting naturalism arose not just from a theological conviction but from a logical one as well.

I now turn to Lewis's specific encounters in the '40s with the naturalistic mind-set of many scientists.

TWO TYPES OF NATURALISM

Ultimately, Lewis was a professor of literature and therefore a specialist in the humanities and not the sciences. His training in, and knowledge of, the natural sciences was modest at best. Therefore, most of his arguments for faith in light of what he names "the Scientific Outlook" take place in philosophy or the arts. He is not countering the mathematics of the Big Bang cosmology of his contemporary at Cambridge, Fred Hoyle, but taking on the materialistic implications of contemporary biology. Yet this may be a strength, because many arguments against Christian faith are presented by scientists as scientific that are really philosophical in character.

Is there more than one form of naturalism? If so, are all forms of naturalism self-defeating? We arrive at a nexus where confusion can arise. Some atheistic commentators may even use this misunderstanding as a rhetorical shell game, treating all naturalism as coterminous and concluding that God cannot exist in light of the advance of science. So I need to make a distinction. Science commits itself to *methodological naturalism* quite rightly. Science, at its core, commits to a method in which scientists look for the interactions, interrelations, and thus causes and effects in the natural world. For example, when scientists ask the question, "What is the boiling point of water?" they keep testing, hypothesizing, testing, and hypothesizing until they find the natural causes for this effect. They conclude that when water at sea level is heated to 100 Celsius, it begins to boil. No god or spirit is needed for that specific phenomenon of nature (other than a Creator God who put together nature itself—but I will return to that theme below). The methods of scientists become complicated in more elaborate theories—quantum theory comes to mind—but the basic commitment to find solely natural causes remains. This is proper methodological naturalism.

The issue is when this method of looking solely for natural causes becomes conflated with *philosophical naturalism*— that all that exists is nature. Just because science cannot test or number something does not mean it does not exist. It is here—not with naturalism as a method of study but as a philosophy to understand the world overall—where science often intersects or even collides with theology. Many atheistic evolutionists use the theory of natural selection and conclude that the natural world of cause and effect is not guided but mindless. Or to be more clear, in the words of Richard Dawkins, "The universe that we observe has precisely the properties we should expect if there is, at bottom, no design, no purpose, no evil and no good, nothing but blind, pitiless indifference."[13]

He sets this view against the purposeful creation by the hand of God. A modern proverb, generally referenced as originating from a sign on Albert Einstein's door, addresses scientists' predilection for numbering and its relation to philosophical naturalism: "Everything that can be counted does not necessarily count; everything that counts cannot necessarily be counted."

And though many scientists and atheistic philosophers casually link methodological naturalism with philosophical atheism, there remains no sound reason to do so. Here a distinction is helpful. There exists a fundamental difference between God and the natural world. Simply put, there is *primary* and *secondary* causation. God is the primary cause—God undergirds and establishes all being. As the great medieval philosopher Thomas Aquinas taught, the nature of God as Creator is that being itself continually flows from the Creator. That fact defines primary causation. Secondary causation is what human beings, and all other agents in the natural world, are given to do. Shakespeare created Hamlet and Ophelia—that is the nature of authorship. They would not exist without him, but within the story they have real interaction. They exist because Shakespeare, as it were, brought them into being. Admittedly, the analogy is not perfect because once the author writes the play, the real interactions between Hamlet and Ophelia are fixed in a way that ours as real secondary agents are not. Nonetheless, the central analogical point lies here: if Shakespeare were to have stopped writing *Hamlet* in the midst of its creation, the entire story would have ceased. And so too with God. God is the primary cause, but we are real secondary causes. If God were to stop creating, we would no longer exist. At the same time, we can study the real interactions among secondary causes in their own right, without direct reference to the first cause.

"THE SCIENTIFIC OUTLOOK"
IN CONTRAST TO SCIENCE

I make these distinctions between primary and secondary causation and between these two types of naturalism because they are consistent with Lewis. I turn then to our first text at hand: "Is Theology Poetry?" It is an oral presentation Lewis made to the Oxford Socratic Club in 1944.[14] Lewis's fascinating lecture (as he is wont to create) does not address science per se, or even strictly evolutionary science, but the use of evolution to create a worldview, one that challenges orthodox Christian accounts of the world. (On a related note, Lewis preferred Henri Bergson's more vitalistic approach over Darwin's. I can attest to this, having seen Lewis's highly marked-up copy of Bergson's *Creative Evolution*.) To repeat: this atheistic challenge confuses methodological naturalism (the basis of evolution) with philosophical naturalism. Or, as it appears in this essay, Lewis distinguishes between science and "the Scientific Outlook." When scientists grasp this distinction, no conflict between science and God need arise prematurely. Now there may be discoveries about creation that raise questions about the Creator, but science by its nature does not have the power and right to say that all that exists is what it studies.

So Lewis held out great hope for science and faith. He held a positive assessment of science. It is worth considering what he puts in the mouth of the devil, Screwtape, in the first letter of the *Screwtape Letters*, the imagined correspondence between that senior devil and a junior devil, Wormwood, on how to tempt a human soul.

> Above all, do not attempt to use science (I mean, the real sciences) as a defense against Christianity. They will positively encourage him to think about realities he can't touch and see. There have been sad cases among the modern physicists.[15]

Lewis's argument here is that real sciences are *philosophically anti-materialistic*, a point that finds agreement with the eminent Cambridge physicist Sir John Polkinghorne; quantum physics now raises up things that we cannot see or touch. Consider the discovery of the existence of quarks: no one can see them directly, but we have to infer their existence because they help explain material reality.

> Well, quarks are, in some sense, unseen realities. Nobody has ever isolated a single quark in the lab. So we believe in them not because we've, even with sophisticated instruments, so to speak, seen them, but because assuming that they're there makes sense of great swaths of physical experience.[16]

In another brief essay, "Dogma and the Universe," Lewis makes a similar connection between modern physics and the defeat of classical materialism with the idea that nature depends on its existence from something else.

> In one respect, as many Christians have noticed, contemporary science has recently come into life with Christian doctrine, and parted company with the classical forms of materialism. If anything emerges clearly from modern physics, it is that nature is not everlasting. The universe had a beginning, and will have an end.[17]

He does note, however, "We should not lean too heavily on this, for scientific theories change."[18]

In his essay, Lewis takes up the question given to him: "Is theology poetry?" (This, of course, is also the title of the talk). He does not seem to enjoy the question as it stands before him, so he refines it to address whether theology is *merely* poetry—that is, discourse we enjoy for its beauty but not for its ability to objectively describe reality. He first of all argues that theology is not merely poetry—it is not really artful enough.

The charge that Theology is mere poetry, if it means that Christians believe it because they find it, antecedently to belief, the most poetically attractive of all world pictures, thus seems to me unplausible in the extreme.[19]

Lewis then analyzes the poetry of "the Scientific Outlook" presented by evolution (and especially H. G. Wells) as a philosophy of progress that gradually and painfully overcomes obstacles. It all begins with a humble collection of inanimate matter that gradually becomes life. Dinosaurs emerge first and then die out, replaced by man, who is also destined to die. This great myth is finally "overwhelmed in ruin."[20] It is a beautiful, tragic myth of man fighting valiantly against the odds but ultimately losing.

Lewis had further criticisms of "the Scientific Outlook" that are worthy of note here—the inherent connection, historically, between the rise of science and the search for magic, both as means to *control nature* and to *make it what human beings want.*

[W]e see at once that [Sir Francis] Bacon and the magicians have the closest possible affinity. Both seek knowledge for the sake of power (in Bacon's words, as 'spouse for fruit' not a 'courtesan for pleasure'), both move in a grandiose dream of days when Man shall have been raised to the performance of "all things possible."[21]

Lewis believed, along with the medieval mind, that the goal of human life is to conform to nature. When, in contrast, we seek to use science or nature to bend it to our will and to make it in our image, then we raise enormous problems and we deceive ourselves.

As a result, Lewis lamented the growth of the machine, of the technological progress that distanced us from nature. This, in fact, represents one more sub-crisis, that of living in a technological world that has distanced us from true, good human values and thus from nature. The reader of Lewis's fiction finds this exemplified in N.I.C.E., the National Institute for

Coordinated Experiments, from *That Hideous Strength*, a depiction I find telling but somewhat overwrought. A better example can be found in one of his most notable poems, "The Future of Forestry," where Lewis describes a world that has forgotten the beauty of the forest and thus of nature in its headlong pursuit of technological advances such as roadways. (I am reminded of the work of Lewis's friend and fellow Inkling, Tolkien, who placed in the hands of Saruman, the evil wizard, the destruction of the forests for the sake of production.)

> How will the legend of the age of trees
> Feel, when the last tree falls in England?
> When the concrete spreads and the town conquers
> The country's heart . . .[22]

All these problems derive from scientific materialism, the assertion that this world is all there is and that science has demonstrated this fact. Lewis looked toward a re-enchantment of the world through myth and story to bring us to a place where we can find joy.

The specific reason Lewis rejected "the Scientific Outlook" lies in the self-defeating nature of the two claims "we can think" and "nature is all there is." Here we come to the key theme of this chapter: "the Scientific Outlook" asserts the truth and reasonableness of its claims without thereby providing a place for reason. Or as Lewis phrased it:

> If minds are wholly dependent on brains, and brains on biochemistry, and biochemistry (in the long run) on the meaningless flux of the atoms, I cannot understand how the thought of those minds should have any more significance than the sound of the wind in the trees.[23]

"The Scientific Outlook" tries to fit reason into an irrational—or maybe even *arational*—world. Lewis concludes that this move is self-defeating.

As an alternative, Lewis discovered in his own life (around his conversions in 1930 and 1931) something he argues here: Belief in a Creator God who endows humanity with reason makes entirely more sense. The divine Logos creates human reason. The primary cause undergirds all secondary causes. Lewis says that is why he does not believe in "the Scientific Outlook" but instead believes in Christianity, which includes reason and science. As he closes the lecture, he writes,

> Christian theology can fit in science, art, morality, and the sub-Christian religions. The scientific point of view cannot fit in any of these things, not even science itself. I believe in Christianity as I believe that the Sun has risen, not only because I see it, but because by it I see everything else.[24]

Lewis believed that Christian theology gave grounds for reason and thus reasoning about what is true. It's a vision of life that makes sense of all experience, and therefore it makes sense of science. (And, as I mentioned above, this simultaneously offers a defense of the miraculous, the supernatural, and the truth of the Bible.) Put another way, if science bets its existence on naturalism, then it will ultimately undermine itself. All this appears in a more sustained argument from the 1947 apologetic work *Miracles*. I will concentrate on the key third chapter, "The Cardinal Difficulty with Naturalism," which he revised for the 1960 edition.

THE ARGUMENT IN MIRACLES

As I mentioned above, Lewis defines naturalism simply as the belief that nature is all there is, and he also provides a more extensive definition in *Miracles*: naturalism is

> the doctrine that only Nature—the whole interlocked system—exists. And if that were true, every thing and event

would, if we knew enough, be explicable without remainder (no *heel-taps*) as a necessary product of the system.[25]

With this he continues the essence of the argument he presented in "Is Theology Poetry?" (and elsewhere)—that in order for reason to exist there must be something greater or "above" (*super* in Latin) and thus there must be *supernature*.

Lewis presents his argument against naturalism to kick away a support for disbelieving in miracles. If there is nothing that supervenes over nature, then miracles are impossible. If there is, however, a supernature, then it, or God, could act in ways contrary to the nexus of cause and effect in the natural world. That is a central reason he argues against naturalism.

Now Lewis's argument against naturalism is reasonably simple. It starts with the premise that

1. Naturalism asserts that all that exists is part of the natural, or material, world of cause and effect.
2. Reason, being a part of all that is, must therefore be a component solely of the natural world.
3. Yet in order for reason to discover truth, it cannot be solely based on natural, or material, cause and effect.
4. Therefore naturalists cannot fit reason into their system.
5. Consequently, we cannot know that materialism is true.

As a result of the well-known (and somewhat infamous) debate with the eminent Oxford philosopher Elizabeth Anscombe at the Socratic Club on February 2, 1948, Lewis conceded that Anscombe had pointed out flaws in his essential argument. He presented changes in the 1960 revision to *Miracles*, noting a key distinction between "cause-effect" and "ground-consequent." She too, according to subsequent reflection, felt that he had admitted problems, noting his "honesty and seriousness" as a philosopher. She did not, however, conclude he was destroyed, as later commentators would assert. My own research revealed the same dynamic. While reading through the original Lewis papers at Oxford's Bodleian Library, I happened upon the minutes of the Socratic Club from that debate, and they present a noticeably objective and even-handed rendering of this discussion with sentences such as this: "Mr. Lewis conceded that his use of 'ground' was ill-advised." Put another way, in line with the nature of academic debate, the two engaged in an energetic dialectic, and Anscombe was up to the task and quite formidable. Lewis was losing and had to concede. In fact, he later offered Anscombe as his successor at the Socratic Club.[26] He didn't enjoy losing, but he was accustomed to this type of repartee in academic discussion.

Nevertheless, some want to make sweeping conclusions about this event. For example, A. N. Wilson, in his biography of Lewis, labored incessantly (and even cooked a few facts) to make Lewis's apologetics look unworthy of serious attention, and he repeats a somewhat tired argument that Lewis retreated from apologetics (such as *Miracles*) to children's literature (i.e., *Narnia*) after this encounter. (Below I will note how Wilson's mind changed significantly a few years ago.) He continues by asserting that Lewis even patterned the evil White Witch of Narnia, Jadis, after Anscombe. I find this suggestion incredibly creative but difficult to take seriously.[27] These, and other similar, assertions are overblown. Still, Lewis stated to his pupil, George Sayer, "I can never write another book of that sort."[28] Indeed, Lewis turned his attention away from rational apologetics to imagination.

I have presented the critical elements of his revised presentation not to engage them directly (others have done so effectively)[29] but to demonstrate the effect this confrontation had on Lewis: he moved away from argument and toward story, from justification toward signification. Or put another way, Lewis moved from contemplation to enjoyment. This is a key distinction that Lewis picked up from Samuel Alexander and that he celebrates as a distinctive new insight in *Surprised by Joy*. To "enjoy" is simply to experience without further reflection. To "contemplate" is to reflect on our experience. So in 1950, when he began the "Narniad," as it is called, he wanted to *enjoy* what reasoning implied (a first-order experience), not *contemplate* reason or think about thinking (a second-order experience).[30]

In sum, the argument against naturalism remains critically important today. Lewis made many winning points, but he realized (a) that others, more well-read and interested in academic philosophy and its developments, needed to take up the argument and (b) that he therefore needed to engage his imaginative and literary interests and acumen elsewhere in the apologetic task.

A FINAL THOUGHT

What has made Lewis a valuable mentor for me is that this argument insulated me from the materialist environment of Berkeley during my undergraduate years even before I felt the full force of the materialists' worldview. Its apologetic force remains surprisingly relevant for today's anti-theistic—I have noted Pinker and Dawkins, but there are many others. I have found myself, as one committed to the glory of scientific insight along with my Christian faith, leaning on Lewis. He does not argue that one must conclude that naturalism is self-defeating, only that it is very likely to be self-defeating. And I have not found a convincing rejoinder, although many have been tried,[31] and the debate shows no signs of abating.[32] It is not exactly an argument for Christian faith, but as Lewis concludes in "Is Theology Poetry?" theism—specifically, the creation of the world by a rational Creator—offers the most persuasive ground for human reason.

Perhaps the best closer for this chapter comes from the pen of Wilson, the brilliant but cranky biographer of Lewis who remained, for decades, a committed atheist. Just a few years ago, he changed his mind. In an April 2009 article, he wrote this about "our bishops and theologians:"

> Sadly, they have all but accepted that only stupid people actually believe in Christianity, and that the few intelligent people left in the churches are there only for the music or believe it all in some symbolic or contorted way which, when examined, turns out not to be belief after all. As a matter of fact, I am sure the opposite is the case and that materialist atheism is not merely an arid creed, but totally irrational. Materialist atheism says we are just a collection of chemicals. It has no answer whatsoever to the question of how we should be capable of love or heroism or poetry if we are simply animated pieces of meat.[33]

That declaration seems in the mode of C. S. Lewis himself. But Lewis did not stop with simply impugning naturalism—a negative accomplishment. He also presented a positive argument for something more than this material world can offer. That is the subject of the next chapter.

Chapter 3

THE CRISIS
OF MEANINGLESSNESS

You have made us for yourself, O Lord,
and our hearts are restless until they rest in you.

Augustine, *Confessions*

ONE OF THE ICONIC EVENTS IN THE LITERATURE OF C. S. LEWIS IS
the moment that Lucy Pevensie pushes through the back of
the wardrobe and into the magical land of Narnia. (For American
readers, it might be important to note that a wardrobe is
the British word for armoire, a type of movable closet.) Lucy
steps inside a wardrobe while exploring the unfamiliar house
of Professor Kirk. She discovers that, as she walks back deeper
into the wardrobe, her arms no longer brush smooth fur coats,
but prickly pine trees; her feet no longer touch wood, but cold,
crunchy snow. Soon she meets the faun Tumnus near a lamp-
stand in the middle of a forest. She has entered a new world.

In this scene, Lewis has executed a brilliant feat of imagination where we see that there's something more to this world, and
this similarly implies that the here and now is not enough for us.
We feel discontented with what the world has to offer.

But what does this mean for us? Speaking with a friend
as I described my work on this book, we mused about

dissatisfaction in life. Since we both love books, he recounted an experience of discontent: "You know when you see that title that you just *know* is going to be perfect? It's going to be the next 'thing.' You can hardly wait to have it in your hands. So you order it online, and when it arrives it's just not what you thought it was going to be. It's an anticlimax. You sit with it for a bit. You wish it were different. And then you remember: no earthly event or thing seems as good as the expectation. . . . Greg, I think *that* experience is a taste of what Lewis is presenting in his argument from desire."

Admittedly, this is a tame example of discontent with the things of this world. And yet this experience of disgruntlement can bubble into a crisis. If we continue to seek meaning in this world, we will never be satisfied. We will move from one experience or thrill to the next.

Lewis knew this sense of poignant longing. He described this as the search for joy (which Lewis frequently capitalizes because he uses it as a technical term). The taste of joy—and the desire it evokes—began early in his life and gradually expanded, like a time-release capsule that drove him to God. This search forms the major theme of both *The Pilgrim's Regress* and *Surprised by Joy*. For Lewis, joy represents an intense longing for something more. Joy is "an unsatisfied desire which is itself more desirable than any other satisfaction."[1] For that reason, he also employed the German term "*Sehnsucht*," which is defined as "longing," "yearning," or more broadly, "intensely missing." Lewis described *Sehnsucht* as the "inconsolable longing" in the human heart for "we know not what." In the afterword to the third edition of *The Pilgrim's Regress*, he provided examples of what sparked this desire in him particularly.

> That unnameable something, desire for which pierces us like a rapier at the smell of bonfire, the sound of wild ducks flying overhead, the title of *The Well at the World's End*, the opening

lines of *Kubla Khan*, the morning cobwebs in late summer, or the noise of falling waves.[2]

I cite this as a reminder that Lewis's imagination was always decidedly literary. I doubt many of Lewis's readers would cite *Kubla Khan* as the moment where we felt that gnawing for something more.

Lewis knew personal moments of such intense longing. For example, Lewis remembered from what he calls the "very early days" of childhood during which his brother, Warren, and he constructed a toy garden on the lid of a biscuit tin. He calls it "the first beauty I ever knew" which was "something cool, dewy, fresh, and exuberant" and led him to *Sehnsucht*. "As long as I live my imagination of Paradise will retain something of my brother's toy garden."[3] Added to this, a view of the Castelreagh Hills from his nursery window, which were "not very far off but . . . to children, quite unattainable."[4] These taught him *Sehnsucht*.

I am stuck on the phrase "my imagination of Paradise." His early experience of joy, or *Sehnsucht*, formed what he would later imagine in his books as the fulfillment of life—in other words, heaven. I need to insert here one quibble with St. Clive. According to several passages in the Bible, such as Revelation 21:1–4, our future is really a "new heaven and a new earth." When he employs the term "heaven," he implies this grander renewal of creation. In any event, this experience of joy and longing also came from a literary source: it occurred when Lewis read his favorite Beatrix Potter book, *Squirrel Nutkin*.[5] Here again Lewis's choice is somewhat idiosyncratic. *Squirrel Nutkin* is a quaint, brief story about a rodent that tantalizes Owl while searching for food, makes Owl angry, and then loses his tail to Owl. It is hard to understand how this simple story could evoke such emotions for Lewis. Nonetheless, however *Sehnsucht* located him, it provided a theme for his life. By this own admission—and as seen in the content of his auto-biographies—Lewis valued these experiences above almost everything else and spent his early life searching for them. He wanted to push back through the wardrobe, and I suspect that is one reason he wrote The Chronicles of Narnia—he also wanted to help children experience this other world before the materialistic culture around them leached out that possibility.

But he also realized that joy, by its nature, cannot be fulfilled here on earth. Here, in his childhood, Lewis found an ache for something more. Though the desire ebbed and flowed, it still sent him on a lifelong quest. Indeed it was his discontentedness that produced the crisis that ultimately led him to God. And Lewis had to resolve this crisis for himself. Is there something beyond this world? The fourth- and fifth-century-BCE Greek philosopher Plato had to resolve this crisis too: he addressed it by asserting the existence of the world of the forms, a place beyond all the things we see in the material world. And in some ways, Lewis loved Plato, probably relating to the sense of longing that his philosophy evokes. But Plato gave Lewis a place to start philosophical exposition about this longing. In my reading, Lewis never fully resolves the Platonist strains in his thought with his Christian belief—especially Plato's teaching that there is a better, perfect world of the "Forms" where there is a perfect form of everything, such as the perfect form of blueness, the perfect form of the chair, and the perfect form of justice. This world is always a pale, imperfect, and unsatisfying copy of the world of perfect forms. My quibble with Lewis is that, from Scripture, we read that God created *this world*, and not from some copy of another world. It is this world that God called "very good" (Gen. 1:31). I will have more to say about Lewis's description of heaven, where his Platonism emerges directly, but for now it should be noted that by concluding that atheistic materialism is self-defeating and incomplete (as the last argument presents), Lewis is also concluding that there is something more. And Plato agreed.

Some, of course, give up the search or consider that the quest for something more is futile. This abandonment of the search is often based on deference to scientific insight. Consider Lewis's early phrase, which I cited in the last apologetic, where he discussed the concept that our brains are composed of a "meaningless flux of the atoms."[6] Lewis realized that this conclusion—the world is meaningless because science has taught us everything is simply a physical system—did not satisfy. For that reason, his argument from desire represents a shrewd move. Thoughtful atheists have also expressed this longing for joy, this *Sehnsucht*, even if they were quite unwilling to follow Lewis's second apologetic. Just a few years before Lewis began formulating this argument, the famous Cambridge philosopher Bertrand Russell expressed a similar longing.

> The centre of me is always and eternally a terrible pain . . . a searching for something beyond what the world contains, something transfigured and infinite—the beatific vision, God—I do not find it, I do not think it is to be found—but the love of it is my life . . . it is the actual spring of life within me.[7]

Russell decided there was no solution except the searching. As Lewis took on what he describes in *Surprised by Joy* as the "New Look," with its implicit realism and scientific atheism, he struggled to include his longing for something more, a longing that he discovered through his literary studies. Another way to put this—as Lewis himself did—is that rationality found itself in a fight-to-the-death with romanticism (which always stood against materialism). Lewis discovered a resolution in his Christian faith.

At this point, I need to be careful. In the full context of Lewis's writings, the relationship between joy and God is curious. Joy in itself, as Lewis defines it, is simply a marker. The value of joy is in the desiring.[8] On the very last page of *Surprised by Joy*, he says the subject of joy "has lost nearly all

interest for me since I became a Christian." He continues—
and I'm adding some italics—by noting the stabs of *Sehnsucht*
still to come. "But I now know that the experience, *considered
as a state of my own mind,* had never had the kind of importance I once gave it. It was valuable only as a pointer to something other and outer."[9] The state of one's mind fades away in
the light of heaven. Lewis's subjective experience has limited
value in the context of God's objective fulfillment. It is like the
gleam of a flashlight in the darkness fading once the sun rises.

So in this second apologetic step is Lewis's argument
from desire, which defines the crisis of meaninglessness. It is
simple, yet potent. I have found this discontentment with the
world and the desire for something more to be well-nigh universal. Lewis embeds this in his comments on the theological
virtue of hope. "Creatures are not born with desires unless
satisfaction for those desires exists." Babies feel hunger for
which there is food. Ducklings want to swim; there is water.
Human beings have sexual desire, and there is sex. "If I find in
myself a desire which no experience in this world can satisfy,
the most probable explanation is that I was made for another
world."[10] Put simply, we have a desire for something that cannot be satisfied by this world, and our hunger demonstrates
that we need something beyond this world. There is more to
this world, and our heart tells us so.

In order to grasp the progression of this argument, I will
next outline that our desires—and thus pleasure—can be
trusted as good. Then I will examine how this desire leads to
glory, how this argument is suppositional, and how well desire
delivers what it promises.

PLEASURE COMES FROM GOD

In order to see how Lewis unfolded this apologetic argument,
we must grasp what is implicit: for Lewis pleasure is ultimately

good because it issues from a God who loves to give good gifts. On the surface, this may strike us as contradictory because almost every use of pleasure we see is contrary to Christian faith. And Christian moralists either warn us about money, sex, and power as things that lure us away from God or secular culture presents the argument that all the best things are sinful.

Lewis moves in an entirely different direction. Lewis is drawing on an older tradition, which he does so effortlessly that the reader might miss how much scholarship lies in the background of his satirical wit in the citation below. (Lewis always carries his considerable scholarship lightly.) This older tradition tells us that God is the ultimate good. The first chapter of the book of James enunciates the connection between goodness and God quite clearly: "Every good gift and every perfect gift is from above, and cometh down from the Father of lights, with whom is no variableness, neither shadow of turning" (1:17). Similarly, in the much older tradition of Psalms, God is the source of beauty because God is beautiful: "And let the beauty of the LORD our God be upon us" (Ps. 90:17). "Out of Zion, the perfection of beauty, God hath shined" (Ps. 50:2). And beauty gives us pleasure. Therefore to know God is to experience what is best and what is most pleasurable. Lewis sets this best in the mouth of the tempter, Screwtape, as he talks about his adversary God as "a hedonist at heart" and "vulgar":

> He has filled His world full of pleasures. There are things for humans to do all day long without His minding in the least—sleeping, washing, eating, drinking, making love, playing, praying, working. Everything has to be *twisted* before it's any use to us. We fight under cruel disadvantages. Nothing is naturally on our side.[11]

Implicit in that word *twisted* is Lewis's understanding of evil—that evil is parasitic of good. As Screwtape puts it: "Everything has to be *twisted* before it's any use to us." Evil can only take what God has created and turn it to purposes for which it was never intended, especially turning us from God. Conversely, good, beauty, joy—and thus pleasure—create a pathway to God when they are enjoyed in the ways God intended.

For that reason, Lewis can argue that God helps us seek true pleasure, and the truest pleasure of all, God Himself, or glory. This, in the famous triad of Platonic transcendentals—good, truth, and beauty—is an apologetic for the beautiful. Good forms us morally. Truth forms our minds. And beauty lures us. It is what we desire. It is what makes truth and goodness desirable and interesting. In some ways, beauty—as a synonym for joy—constitutes the goal of human life. As he phrases this in his magnificent sermon, "The Weight of Glory," preached at the stunning Oxford University Church of St. Mary the Virgin on June 8, 1942:

> We do not want merely to *see* beauty, though, God knows, even that is bounty enough. We want something else which can hardly be put into words—to be united with the beauty we see, to pass into it, to receive it into ourselves, to bathe in it, to become part of it. [12]

This desire for beauty leads to our feeling of emptiness. Because there is something more, and that inkling of something more gnaws at us. But it also contains the promise of glory.

DESIRE LEADS TO GLORY

As Lewis preaches "The Weight of Glory" to a packed congregation of Oxford undergraduates, he describes his own discovery: at first he was shocked to find that celebrated Christian writers as different as John Milton and Thomas Aquinas depicted heavenly glory as approval by God. Lewis had rejected this previously as simplistic, but when he took in this connection—that to be delighted in by God "as an artist delights in his work or a father in a son" that indeed represents "a weight or burden of glory," and this realization similarly resolved for him the relationship between desire and glory:

> Glory, as Christianity teaches me to hope for it, turns out to satisfy my original desire and indeed to reveal an element in that desire which I had not noticed. . . . welcome into the heart of all things. The door on which we have been knocking all our lives will open at last.[13]

This longing for something greater leads us to desire its consummation. Joy leads to glory. Or as "the Teacher" in *The Great Divorce*, George MacDonald, says, "No soul that seriously and constantly desires joy will ever miss it."[14] Our yearning for something more will be satisfied by God's promise of heaven.

Conversely, to reject joy is to live in hell, as the Dwarf does in *The Great Divorce* even when beckoned toward the joy of heaven by his wife on earth, Sarah Smith, who could "waken all dead things of the universe into life"[15] with her unmitigated joy. In addressing the topic of heaven and hell, I have ventured into territory that I will concentrate on later in chapter 9, but for now, we must recognize that the argument from desire leads to its fulfillment beyond this world. It is the direction this line of reasoning takes us. Without it, Lewis's second apologetic step is truncated.

IMAGINATION AND SUPPOSITION

How does this argument work? I offer myself as Exhibit A for engaging with this crisis of meaninglessness. As I searched for meaning in the first year of college, I *knew* at some level that there had to be more. There had to be something beyond this material world. And in Lewis I met a fellow discoverer. This brings me to something his friend and colleague at Oxford, the philosopher Austin Farrer, wrote about Lewis: "We think we are listening to an argument, in fact we are presented with a vision; and it is the vision that carries conviction."[16] This kind of argument works for many because of Lewis's formidable imagination. For that reason, it is a literary more than a philosophical argument. It draws, as it were, more from Lewis's degree in literature than his studies in ancient philosophy. Here, although Lewis employs his profound analytical skills, it draws most on his creativity.

It is important here to recall his preaching in the university chapel on that hot July day in 1945:

> In speaking of this desire for our own far-off country, which we find in ourselves even now, I feel a certain shyness. I am almost committing an indecency. I am trying to rip open the inconsolable secret in each one of you—the secret which hurts so much that you take your revenge on it by calling it names like Nostalgia and Romanticism and Adolescence.[17]

Lewis wants to awaken our desire and imagination. For this reason, he is not presenting a deductive argument that begins with general premises and makes specific conclusions: "All men are mortal. Socrates is a man. Therefore Socrates is mortal." Lewis would have learned that in the first weeks of his degree program in Greats (or ancient philosophy), but it is not the form of this apologetic. If we are expecting a logical, deductive argument, we will be disappointed. Sadly, I have often heard Lewis presented as one more logical (at least, in this deductive sense, "logical") apologist. It is simply not his approach. Instead of the deduction employed in his argument against naturalism (the previous chapter), his other apologetic arguments are better seen as a *supposition* (or alternatively, argument to the best explanation).

A supposition, first of all, is not allegory. When Lewis described what he was doing with Narnia, he steadfastly denied that these stories were allegories, where each particular character or other element in the story bears an exact one-to-one correspondence with a concept. Here I'm thinking of Lewis's own *The Pilgrim's Regress*, but even more of John Bunyan's landmark *The Pilgrim's Progress*, where the pilgrim, Christian, meets the Slough of Despair, which not surprisingly has a one-to-one correspondence with facing despair in the Christian life. Or Lewis points to the giant who represents despair:

> If Aslan represented the immaterial Deity in the same way in which Giant Despair represents Despair, he would be an allegorical figure. In reality however he is an invention giving an imaginary answer to the question, "What might Christ become like if there really were a world like Narnia and He chose to be incarnate and die and rise again in *that* world as He actually has done in ours?" This is not an allegory at all. So in "Perelandra." This works out a *supposition*.[18]

Lewis is creating a supposition, not an allegory or logically deductive argument. Indeed, as the citation above suggests, the basis of this argument is imagination. As an apologetic argument, it is an imaginative one. And that makes it more powerful because it baptizes our imagination, just as George MacDonald's *Phantastes* baptized Lewis's imagination in February 1916.

Consider another example from *Miracles*, where Lewis is presenting a case for the "Grand Miracle," the Incarnation of Jesus Christ. I'll add italics for emphasis:

> Let us *suppose* we possess parts of a novel or a symphony. Someone now brings us a newly discovered piece of manuscript and says, "This is the missing part of the work. This is the chapter on which the whole plot of the novel really turned. This is the main theme of the symphony."[19]

The test of its genuineness is whether it gives light to all the other parts. Does it pull them together? If it doesn't pull the parts together, it's spurious. But if this new chapter or section removes difficulties in other places and gives fresh insight to other details, it must be genuine. The same is true for the Incarnation, the Grand Miracle, which, as a part of his larger case in *Miracles*, makes sense of the miraculous generally.

> The credibility will depend on the extent to which the doctrine, if accepted, can illuminate and integrate that whole mass. It is much less important that the doctrine itself should be fully comprehensible.[20]

And then Lewis continues with one of his characteristic analogies that simultaneously illuminates this suppositional form of argument. It does not *deduce* the central conclusion to demonstrate its truth. Instead, the central conclusion remains a bit inaccessible directly, except insofar as it illuminates the entire landscape of the argument.

> We believe that the sun is in the sky at midday in summer not because we can clearly see the sun (in fact, we cannot) but because we can see everything else.[21]

And so too the argument from desire: it is based on a supposition. We do not fully understand the desire itself, but it points to a wider metaphysical conclusion, one that in turn points to God, who created us. Or more systematically, the form of this suppositional argument from desire proceeds as follows: *supposing* God created this world, we can imagine that God would leave a desire for more than this world offers. We experience a longing for more than this world offers; it is reasonable to see this as a pointer to God.

EVALUATION

But does this argument convince us? I argued above for this longing, this *Sehnsucht*. For readers of John Calvin, this sounds a great deal like his "sense of divinity" (or *sensus divinitatis* in Latin). In Calvin's vastly influential 1559 *Institutes of the Christian Religion*, he wrote, "There is within the human mind, and indeed by natural instinct, an awareness of divinity."[22] It is akin to Augustine's restlessness that I quoted at the beginning of the chapter. Undoubtedly this awareness of divinity is vague and can be open to manipulation—it can lead to a narcissistic devotion to the "God within" or the Nazi conviction that God is working through the German culture and *Volk*, but this *sensus divinitatis* also provides an important function in opening us up to God. It plays a similar role as Lewis continues to build his four-part apologetic.

Surprisingly enough—because Lewis had deep concerns about science and its misuse, as I illustrated in the previous chapter—contemporary cognitive science offers stunning support for Lewis's concept of *Sehnsucht* or joy. For example, neuroscientist Justin Barrett, through his work in developing a Cognitive Science of Religion, uses the findings of the cognitive sciences to argue that evolution has developed human beings so that we implicitly see purposes in events or are predisposed toward teleology. "Evidence exists that people are also prone to see the world as purposeful and intentionally ordered,"[23] which naturally leads to belief in a Creator. For example, preschoolers "are inclined to see the world as purposefully designed *and* tend to see an intelligent, intentional agent as behind this natural design."[24] Barrett notes that there are similarities this shares with John Calvin's *sensus divinitatis,* pointing to a sense of the numinous, powerful and brooding. "Whither shall I go from thy spirit? or whiter shall I flee from thy presence?" cries the psalmist in Psalm 139. It is the feeling of being out in a forest at night, knowing that no one is there but feeling *something*. Often this experience can frighten us, and yet it also provides a witness to the natural knowledge of God.

To take a more prosaic view, consider the massively popular song "Somewhere Over the Rainbow": this is where any dreams that we have dared to dream really do come true.[25] And additional examples for this are legion. What is powerful about this apologetic is that it doesn't take Scripture to evoke these thoughts. They lie close. The question is whether we relate joy and *Sehnsucht* to God or, indeed, anything except wishful thinking.

Atheists use this longing to impugn belief in God. In other words, suppose there is no God, and evolution has created our brains so that we cannot help but believe. Therefore no God exists. God is simply in our brains. We may *feel* and *wish for* something more. But nothing is out there. Indeed, there is no irrefutable argument for God, and there are many reasons we resist. Lewis sets before us a choice, and he wants to make that choice attractive through his imaginative supposition. All this is reminiscent of what the famous seventeenth-century scientist, philosopher, and Christian Blaise Pascal wrote:

> Men despise religion. They hate it and are afraid it may be true. The cure for this is first to show that religion is not contrary to reason, but worthy of reverence and respect. Next make it attractive, make good men wish it were true, and then show that it is.[26]

So I, joining Lewis, argue that if we suppose there is a God, the findings of cognitive neuroscience help us see that this sense of divinity is a witness to God as our Creator. We are created with openness to belief, and joy is its signpost.

But it is not our only signpost. Lewis closely related this theme of *Sehnsucht* with the God who gives us a sense of right and wrong. The house of heaven evokes the master architect because the architect cannot literally show up in the house, but we can know him through the design:

> If there was a controlling power outside the universe, it could not show itself to us as one of the facts inside the universe— no more than the architect of a house could actually be a wall

or staircase or fireplace in that house. The only way in which we could expect it to show itself would be inside ourselves as an influence or a command trying to get us to behave in a certain way. And that is just what we do find inside ourselves.[27]

This brings us to the argument from the moral law, Lewis's third apologetic step and the topic of the following chapter.

Chapter 4

THE CRISIS OF ANOMIE

Question: *Of Lewis's arguments,*
which one was the most difficult for you to dispute?

Francis Collins: . . . *Lewis argues that if you are looking for evidence of*
a God who cares about us as individuals, where could you more likely look
than within your own heart at this very simple concept of what's right and
what's wrong. And there it is. Not only does it tell you something about
the fact that there is a spiritual nature that is somehow written within our
hearts, but it also tells you something about the nature of God himself,
which is that he is a good and holy God. What we have there is a glimpse of
what he stands for.

From PBS, *The Question of God*

C. S LEWIS WAS MOTIVATED TO RESOLVE VARIOUS CRISES IN HIS
life because he desired joy. One crisis he encountered was this:
we cannot discover joy unless we live according to the moral
design of the universe. I can't help but see that this argument
is connected with what Lewis faced when he first started at
Oxford. There he realized that there were other men that chal-
lenged his cavalier attitude toward the moral life, "when," as he
writes in *The Problem of Pain*, "the man of inferior moral standards enters the society of those who are better and wiser than
he and gradually learns to accept *their* standards—a process
which, as it happens, I can describe fairly accurately, since I have
undergone it."[1] In *Surprised by Joy*, he recounts meeting these
students who truly tried to practice good ethics. "They were all,

by decent Pagan standards (much more, by so low a standard as mine), 'good.'"[2] I suspect this opened him to see that morality was important and that there was a sense in which all believed in its importance. In addition, when he became a theist a decade later, he realized that inside him was a "a zoo of lusts, a bedlam of ambitions, a nursery of fears, a harem of fondled hatreds. My name was legion."[3] In sum, he discovered both that there was a moral law practiced by those of no revealed religious ethics and simultaneously that he did not live up to that law.

Moreover, I have read and reread records of Lewis's life and their speculations on the existence of an affair between him and Mrs. Moore. These accounts consider him as a lonely, atheist twenty-something inevitably feeling the ache of a truncated relationship with his mother and suggest that he sexualized these longings and began an affair with Mrs. Moore, perhaps in the summer of 1918. If so, Lewis broke off this affair, I believe, when he became a Christian—one possible reason Mrs. Moore rejected his Christian faith. I fully admit that nothing definitive on this exists in his writing, but we can unearth some clues. "When I came first to the University, I was as nearly without a moral conscience as a boy could be . . . of chastity, truthfulness and self-sacrifice, I thought as a baboon thinks of classical music."[4] Ultimately, my conclusion about his relationship with Mrs. Moore arises from knowing Lewis through his books for decades and leaning on his biographers. All this is to say that, in one way or another, Lewis found that our sense of right and wrong offers a clue to the existence of a moral God, that we break this law, and that anomie in his own life created crises for him. And so we arrive at the third part of his apologetic strategy.

THE ARGUMENT FROM THE MORAL LAW

For these reasons, it's not entirely a surprise that in his most famous apologetic book—and probably the most famous apologetic book in the twentieth century, *Mere Christianity*[5]—Lewis begins as follows:

> Every one has heard people quarrelling. Sometimes it sounds funny and sometimes it sounds merely unpleasant; but however it sounds, I believe we can learn something very important from listening to the kind of things they say. They say things like this: "How'd you like it if anyone did the same to you?"—"That's my seat, I was there first"—"Leave him alone, he isn't doing you any harm."[6]

Lewis points to a common stock of morals and concludes we often don't live up to these moral codes: "we have failed to practice ourselves the kind of behavior we expect from other people."[7] Lewis's essential argument is that all people have a common stock of morality. Of course, this is what Christian tradition has long found in Paul's words about the non-Jews or Gentiles:

> For when the Gentiles, which have not the law, do by nature the things contained in the law, these, having not the law, are a law unto themselves: Which shew the work of the law written in their hearts, their conscience also bearing witness. (Rom. 2:14–15)

The universe is moral and our conscience tells us so. The reality of this common stock of morals offers a clue that there is a good God who gave us this moral sense.

This apologetic approach has proven remarkably resilient and effective. Charles Colson's response provides one notable example of Lewis's effectiveness, as well as the way his work resolved a profound personal crisis. During Watergate and thus the related crises he faced, Colson visited a friend and successful businessman, Tom Phillips, who had himself converted to Christianity. On a hot summer night in 1973, Phillips prayed with Colson and read him a passage from *Mere Christianity* about what Lewis named the great sin, pride. Colson recounted this experience as his life "flashed before" him. Although he thought he had been driven to be good to his family, to build a good law firm, and to be a patriot; instead, as Colson wrote, his work all those years was about "feeding my pride, proving how good I was" and thus "I had missed the real pinnacle—to know God in a personal way."[8] Having lost his integrity years before to Washington politics and specifically to Nixon's campaign for reelection, his pride had been broken, and he now surrendered himself to God. Colson, who was to call his autobiography *Born Again*,[9] later sat in his car weeping with tears of relief. As a result, Colson treasured *Mere Christianity* and distributed hundreds of copies: "It is the book God has used most powerfully in my life, apart from his own Word."[10] Colson's response to *Mere Christianity,* and particularly his conversion, points to his conviction that he violated a natural moral law—through grasping the sin of pride. It exemplifies the first of Lewis's apologetic arguments.

To summarize, the basic argument for God runs as follows: The existence of our moral sense (our ability to decide between right and wrong) points to the divine Lawgiver, a God who cares about morality. These are "clues to the meaning of the universe," as Lewis titles book 1 of *Mere Christianity*. Similar to the argument from desire, this does not constitute a deductive argument that proceeds from universal, general propositions to inexorable conclusions. Instead, the argument from morality is a supposition that presents the best explanations for the world—and ourselves. In other words, *suppose* a moral God exists; we can then imagine a world in which our sense of objective morality would correspond to that mortality. This sense of objective morality exists. Therefore it is reasonable, even the best explanation of ourselves and our world, to conclude that this God exists.

Lewis believed that our moral sense is also necessitated by the Christian faith. If Jesus calls us to repent, as he does in the beginning of the Gospels (for example, Mark 1:15, "repent ye, and believe the gospel"), then we must have a moral compass that leads us to repentance. Lewis summarized the argument and its importance in *Mere Christianity*:

> First . . . human beings, all over the earth, have this curious idea that they ought to behave in a certain way, and cannot really get rid of it. Secondly . . . they do not in fact behave in that way. They know the Law of Nature; they break it. These two facts are the foundation of all clear thinking about ourselves and the universe we live in.[11]

We all have this moral sense. Therefore Jesus did not have to invent something new when he preached.

Like any of his major ideas, Lewis reworked this theme in several books. He flipped it around and set it into the imagined correspondence between devils in *The Screwtape Letters*. The older and more experienced Screwtape tells Wormwood about how to distract human beings from seeing that Jesus's words agreed with most other moral teachers. Ironically, they must first depict Jesus as

> solely a teacher, and then conceal the very substantial agreement between His teachings and those of all other great moral teachers. For humans must not be allowed to notice that all great moralists are sent by the Enemy not to inform men but to remind them, to restate the primeval moral platitudes against our continual concealment of them.[12]

Jesus draws his listeners—and us—*back* to what we already know. In that sense, he is at least a great moral teacher like other teachers of the Way (as Lewis names it in *The Abolition of Man*) or the moral law.

It is worth noting that Lewis believed in objective morality—that right and wrong in the universe is not simply a subjective decision that we individually, or as societies, make; instead morality exists outside us, within our world. We live according to the way the world objectively exists when we live morally. "It is the doctrine of objective value, the belief that certain attitudes are really true, and others really false, to the kind of thing the universe is and the kind of things we are."[13] To falsify this claim, one has to merely demonstrate that moralities among various cultures radically diverge. Thus, to prove it true, Lewis had to provide cross-cultural and trans-temporal examples. He also argued that the differences in the moral law are minor and that therefore we can conclude that the moral law is really like math: there is a standard, but we may be closer or farther from that standard. Lewis worked hard to support this approach in *The Abolition of Man* in the form that it would have been presented in the mid-century—that personal choices tell us more about the subject than the object. He argues that, until recently, a wide range of cultures believed in the Way or the Tao. Lewis concludes this book with a relatively lengthy comparative list of moral codes across a wide range of cultures, ranging from Babylonian, Ancient Egyptian, Old Norse, ancient Jewish, Hindu, Chinese, Stoic, and Christian.[14]

MORAL REALISM IN NARNIA

As is typical of Lewis, he wanted *to show as well as tell*. In his language, he wanted us to *enjoy* as well as *contemplate*. For that reason, especially in the 1950s, he turned to fiction. His argument about moral law meets the moral universe of The Chronicles of Narnia.

One key characteristic of the land of Narnia is Lewis's creation of a profoundly moral universe. The good are ultimately rewarded; evil can be redeemed, but unrepentant evil does not win out. There is a corresponding remarkable lack of irony in Narnia—colloquially, it lacks our postmodern sensibility of "whatever," of a world where no one is ultimately committed to moral good because all morality disappears in the murky contours of human action. Instead, in *The Lion, the Witch, and Wardrobe,* for example, Peter, Lucy, and Susan gain favor through their moral courage. They are rewarded with leadership as kings and queens. (I use the passive voice here because it seems as if moral realism is wound into Narnia itself.) I omitted Edmund in the list above because his case demonstrates a different but even greater good—the redemption of the evildoer. Though he commits the horrendous sin of betraying Aslan—and this ultimately causes Aslan's murder at the hands of Jadis—Edmund becomes wiser and stronger and takes on the name Edmund the Just. Finally, in this universe of objective morality, evil will not triumph: Jadis, who rules Narnia with evil magic and totalitarian terror, is killed in battle. Evil that cannot receive redemption is destroyed.

If all this sounds quite Christian, it should. The moral realism of Narnia corresponds to Lewis's imaginative tutelage through the literature of the largely Christian Middle Ages— and I mean Christian in the sense of worldview and moral vision, not necessarily in behavior. The world of medieval literature, which Lewis inhabited out of love but also studied as a professor at both Oxford and Cambridge, follows the arc of the Christian story: God creates with good intention. Human evil mars creation. Reality seems to be overwhelmed by evil until ultimate good triumphs. One can see this narrative arc through the seven stories of *Narnia,* with its completion in *The Last Battle*—similar in grandeur to the final battle in Tolkien's The Lord of the Rings trilogy. As Tolkien would describe it, this is the "eucatastrophe"—at the last minute, and against all odds, good will triumph.

Lewis's moral universe also contrasts markedly with his experience in the chaotically immoral universe of boarding school. One telling example is the sadistic schoolmaster at Wynyard, the Reverend Robert Capon. But there are many more that Lewis describes in exhausting—to my mind, disproportionately—detail in *Surprised by Joy.* The importance of a moral universe explains Lewis's repulsion at his years of boarding school, which for him signified a world where adults live immorally and chaotically, and the children can do nothing about it. As a child Lewis implored his father to remove him from this hell. His efforts were unsuccessful for six years until he was finally tutored by the beloved William Kirkpatrick. Lewis was deeply convinced that this world was evil and would not triumph. This was a welcome and necessary change because his psychological sanity depended on it. In fact, the crisis of the anomie of boarding schools illuminates why Lewis turned to writing fiction about children who live in a profoundly moral world largely outside of adult power. It also gives us some clue as to why moral realism matters to Lewis. He not only argued for it in *Mere Christianity* and *The Abolition of Man*, but he also imaginatively portrayed it in The Chronicles of Narnia. Finally, and as I have argued throughout, writing out the resolution of this crisis of anomie speaks to our crises, since we often find ourselves today in a world that seems chaotic and profoundly immoral.

EVALUATION

Sometimes when I've taught this material on moral realism in Lewis's writing, students can barely restrain their enthusiastic agreement with Lewis. They nod in conscious agreement. Others wonder how with the vast differences among cultures—of which we are quite conscious—this universality morality can be maintained. So what are we to make of Lewis's argument today? As I read the contemporary climate, this argument receives two diametrically opposed responses. Both of these, incidentally, appear in *Mere Christianity*.

First of all, the relativistic postmodernist asserts that all behavior is either culturally relative, a matter of personal preference, or the result of other forces not related to a universal law of right and wrong. For example, Michel Foucault, who was the secular pope of philosophy in my undergraduate years, and Frederick Nietzsche before him, believed that morality is simply about power.[15] What is right and good is determined by whoever defines the discourse, i.e., whoever has the power. Therefore morality is variable, relative, and not at all universal. In *Mere Christianity*, Lewis comments that some readers have questioned whether this universal moral law isn't just social convention, which itself is the result of education. Lewis responded with the assertion that, just because we receive ideas through education, it doesn't mean they are culturally variable. Mathematics does not depend on our teachers. They are "real truths," but the side of the road we use for driving might vary. They are "mere conventions." The laws of human behavior are in the first category.[16]

Supporting Lewis's argument for moral realism, or an objective standard of morality, has is an interesting new advocate in some circles of evolutionary theory. These voices emphasize the importance of what is called "prosocial behavior" as a way that human beings have flourished. Both David Sloan Wilson and Justin Barrett have argued in different ways that it makes sense, evolutionarily, for human beings to collaborate even more than to compete.[17] Barrett has noted that this area of research suggests that evolutionary pressures, particularly the human tendency toward cooperation as it leads to survival, produces a common stock of morality; "a recurring theme is that humans seem to naturally converge upon a common set of intuitions that structure moral thought," such as "it is wrong to harm a nonconsenting member of one's group."[18] I remember hearing Wilson, an evolutionary biologist, offer this question at a conference (and I paraphrase): "You put two groups on a desert island. One is completely self-centered. The other has learned to work as a team, to cooperate, sometimes taking less so that others will survive. Which of the two groups is going to survive the longest—the self-seeking or the altruistic?" Obviously, it's those who cooperate. They will have bonded together against various foes and become stronger. So if we are altruistic in the sense that Wilson describes, it's good common sense: we are more likely to survive. Here Lewis has a ally, and he called this concept "the herd instinct"[19] to show its connection with the way natural selection formed this behavior. As long as we can maintain some commitment to dual causation—as I've noted in chapter 2, that God, as primary cause, works through natural secondary causes—we have no reason to doubt the conclusion that God could use the forces of evolution to bring about moral reasoning. In fact, it makes abundant sense: if our world is morally formed, there is an increasing fitted-ness to our environment the more we act morally. Just as an eye evolves because light really exists, so also our moral sense evolves because right and wrong really exist.

So I find support for Lewis's argument from a contemporary ethics based on evolutionary theory. Moreover, my own evaluation of this argument from natural law begins by paraphrasing Farrer's profound insight on Lewis: we are not simply hearing an argument; we are presented with a vision that carries conviction. And Lewis is convinced that moral formation is central to human life and happiness. We are happiest, most fully alive, when we live in accordance with the moral universe God has created. In this light, even suffering has a purpose. I will address this much more in chapter 8, but I will offer one question here: How did Lewis ultimately resolve the problem of evil's existence while maintaining that God is good? We are in need of moral formation, and pain can form us. If all this sounds entirely harsh, it's worth nothing that moral formation for Lewis is not in the simplistic sense of being a do-gooder. As he put it: we might begin by thinking that Christianity seems all about morality, "all about duties and rules and guilt and virtue, yet it leads you on, out of all that, into something beyond . . . a country where they do not talk of those things, except perhaps as a joke"[20] because they are looking at the source from which it comes, God. So moral formation leads us to Beatific Vision. It leads us to be the kind of people that can bear the weight of glory—and if this sounds like character formation along the lines of Aristotle's virtue ethics, it ought to.

Therefore, I'm a bit divided on the effectiveness of this argument from contemporary science—for those who believe in a common stock of morality (such as the evolutionary folks), it makes sense. God used natural forces to create this natural morality. And yet, I would add, with Francis Collins, that sometimes we act against our evolutionary instincts because those direct us to care solely about our in-group. As Collins asks, what about those people who give themselves to a cause beyond their own genes? What about Oskar Schindler? Why did this Nazi-party German save Jews at his own peril?[21] Lewis, in fact, believed that the moral law represented something of a third voice that mediated between these competing voices. God informed this world morally in ways that lie beyond strictly material forces. That, too, makes sense to me: God has surely created natural means to form us morally (largely through evolutionary pressues), but natural forces alone do not exhaust the formation of meaning. God must implant those within his creation and thus within us all. In other words, naturalism is not in itself complete. The natural world needs an informer.

When we grasp the reality of the law of right and wrong, we become wise because our behavior can conform to the way the world is actually created. This is the biblical definition of wisdom—perfecting the skill of doing what's right, what makes sense, and what works. And this returns us the theme that Lewis was ultimately a practical rather than a speculative thinker, and this is what makes Lewis a profoundly morally wise author. Lewis learned much from Aristotle, who would call this skill *phronesis* or practical knowledge. That's why Lewis represents a voice worth paying attention to in our crises, which so often present decisions that require wise, skillful action.

This brings me to a personal note: Lewis's words on pride in *Mere Christianity* didn't so much resolve a crisis as create a crisis for me. And so, in the second quarter of my first year at UC Berkeley, almost three years after reading this for the first time, I decided that I was proud, that I had to replace this idolatry of myself, and that Jesus was indeed the Son of God. I confessed faith in him. Lewis called himself "the most dejected and reluctant convert in all England"; I was more surprised and fearful. I knew that my fraternity brothers would ridicule me and my university professors' post-Christian erudition would subtly mock my gangly, adolescent belief. I sought to kill my self-destructive pride by submitting to God. This also opened me to that critically important virtue of humility, which in turn opened me to learning at a formative time (because I didn't know it all) and to healthy relationships (because I didn't have to compete with others). For whatever it's worth, Lewis's comments on pride played an important role in my own turn toward faith—as they did for Colson—since they struck right at the core secular value, which we sometimes pass off as "self-esteem," but which is really something different. Pride is thinking I'm something special, someone better than others. As Lewis said: "Pride always means enmity—it is enmity. And not only enmity between man and man, but enmity to God."[22]

I typed this section up one day while I was working at Starbucks, and I glanced up and noticed my younger, and incredibly hipper, friend Nate at the table next to me sipping black coffee. He asked what I was writing, and I told him about Lewis and the law of nature and that my thesis revolves around how Lewis's crises meet our crises. He exclaimed, "That's what happened to me!" A few years ago, he had been sexually involved with his girlfriend, which he felt guilty about. She became pregnant, and they decided to put the baby up for adoption. This produced a severe crisis—he had not lived up to the standards of his conscience. He then read *The Problem of Pain* and *Mere Christianity*, and through these books, Lewis helped him resolve his crisis in several ways: through his wise counsel, through the moral vision of his writing, and specifically through showing Nate that the pain of repenting wasn't bad, but necessary. Through Lewis's writings, Nate found resolution to his crisis and returned to faith.

The argument for the natural law and against anomie was personal for Lewis. It was also personal for Nate. Lewis presented this argument as a resolution to the crisis of atheism—how can atheism explain this common stock of moral norms? It leads his listener to see the reasonableness of the Christian vision of life. But there is one more step. From this point, Lewis makes a turn that takes him in a specifically Christian direction: he moves from the God who brings the moral law to the One who comes in person—who is not simply a good moral teacher, but the incarnate God of joy and the moral life, Jesus Christ.

The Crises of Christian Faith

Chapter 5

JESUS AND THE
CRISIS OF OTHER MYTHS

If we regard the Spirit of God as the sole fountain of truth,
we shall neither reject the truth itself, nor despise it wherever it shall appear,
unless we wish to dishonor the Spirit of God.

John Calvin, *Institutes of the Christian Religion*

TWO REALITIES LIE AT THE CENTER OF CHRISTIAN FAITH: JESUS
Christ and the Bible. These represent two quite different categories, but both are critical and are two of the most problematic teachings for C. S. Lewis and his contemporary readers. The second, believing that the Bible is in some way the Word of God, flies in the face of progress. What writing can still give insight today? Moreover, in a culture of videos and the Internet, why trust a written *book* of all things? That second topic I will take up in the next chapter when I look at Lewis's view of the Bible. It is a topic, as a lover and professor of literature, he had to resolve.

But first, "mere Christianity" presents Jesus as unique among other religious figures, and this claim initiated a crisis that moved Lewis from being a theist to a confessing and communicating Christian (by which I mean that he took Communion regularly) on Christmas Day in 1931. Jesus offended his pluralistic sensibilities. He offends ours. Here is a simple test:

Contrast the claim of Jesus's uniqueness with the core Christian virtue of love—a virtue that few would argue against. "I'm not a Christian, but I agree with many of its teaching. Isn't the core of Christianity: Jesus's call to love?" But quote John 14:6 that "No man cometh unto the Father, but by me" and you will receive heaps of scorn about being judgmental. The common phrase "I'm spiritual, but I'm not religious" can mean, among other things, "I accept a lot of what Jesus says, but not his unique place as *the* Son of God." Lewis himself, in his tart, pretentious, early atheist days, wrote to his pious friend, Arthur Greeves,

> That the man Yeshua or Jesus did actually exist, is as certain as that the Buddha did actually exist: Tacitus mentions his execution in the Annals. But all the other tomfoolery about virgin birth, magic healing, apparitions and so forth is on exactly the same footing as any other *mythology*.[1]

I had to italicize the word "mythology" because Lewis—a lover of various myths since his teen years—had to resolve the crisis of answering the essential question, "Who is Jesus Christ?" by making sure he wasn't simply one more mythical figure.

Lest this seems unique to the twenty-first century, there is nothing new about pluralism as context for Christian faith. It came along with the emergence of the message of Christ. The New Testament is written in a stunning array of religious pluralism. I think of the altar to the unknown god in the Areopagus that Paul addressed in Acts 17, the worship of the great Artemis in Ephesus in Acts 19, and the adoration of Aphrodite in Corinth that stands behind Paul's letters to the Corinthians. And that's just a start. New Testament Christians had a variety of religious options in addition to Jesus. It's no wonder that Paul began his letter to the Corinthians with, "But we preach Christ crucified, unto the Jews a stumbling block, and unto the Greeks foolishness" (1 Cor. 1:23).

Lewis did not enjoy the thought of becoming a Christian or even a theist. He knew he would be scorned by the Oxford intellectuals that surrounded him. Actually, at the time of his Christian conversion in 1931, he didn't realize the extent of these rebuffs; his Christian faith—as well as his famous books, like *The Screwtape Letters* and *Mere Christianity*, defending it— would prevent him from receiving a professorship at Oxford. As his colleague at Oxford, Helen Gardner, later commented in the obituary of Lewis she wrote for the British Academy, there was a suspicion that Lewis was so committed to "hot-gospelling" that he would have little time for teaching and that "a good many people thought that shoemakers should stick to their lasts and disliked the thought of a professor of English Literature winning fame as an amateur theologian."[2] So Lewis was never a professor, but instead a *don*, at Oxford. It was Cambridge that finally offered him a chair in 1954.

Lewis certainly knew that orthodox Christian belief was not (as we would say) "politically correct." Moreover, he carried his own doubts. As a lover of myths and their panoply of gods and goddesses, affirming the uniqueness of Christ seemed silly. How then did he resolve this crisis of Christian faith? And how do we believe in the uniqueness of Christ when there are so many religions? Put another way—the way Lewis so often encountered this crisis—since the myths of dying and rising gods share common characteristics with the story of Jesus, aren't they all the same, and therefore there's nothing unique about Jesus?[3]

And so we have arrived at Lewis's fourth apologetic step. Having reasoned that naturalism is self-defeating (step one), he then contended that we desire something more than this world can offer (step two) and that by nature we have a sense of right and wrong that leads us to believe in the God who gives us this law (step three). In this final apologetic Lewis poses the question, Who is Jesus Christ? He asserts that Jesus is either liar, Lord, or lunatic. This is his most famous argument but probably the least elaborated of the four. I'll look first at how this resolves one of Lewis's central crises.

LEWIS'S WALK WITH TOLKIEN AND DYSON

I can imagine the thirty-two-year-old Lewis walking that memorable September 1931 Saturday night in Oxford with his colleagues Hugo Dyson and J. R. R. Tolkien. They circled around the mile or so loop of Addison's Walk through the trees near Lewis's offices at Magdalen, pondering the truth of myths and engaging in dialectic with one another (we would say "arguing") until 4 a.m. The conversation was decisive for Lewis. In a letter to his boyhood friend Arthur Greeves, he admitted that his struggle was between pagan myths—which, as a lover of classical literature, he cherished—and the uniqueness of the story of Jesus:

> Now what Dyson and Tolkien showed was this: that if I met the idea of sacrifice in a Pagan story I didn't mind it at all: that if I met the idea of a god sacrificing himself to himself . . . I liked it very much and was mysteriously moved by it: again, that the idea of the dying and reviving god (Balder, Adonis, Bacchus) similarly moved me provided I met it anywhere *except* in the Gospels.[4]

But on this particular walk in Oxford, which lasted until early in the morning, these two fellow academics demonstrated something new. This was a turning point, or what I've termed a crisis, for Lewis:

> Now the story of Christ is simply a true myth: a myth working in us in the same way as the others, but with this tremendous difference that *it really happened*: and one must be content to accept it in the same way, remembering that it is God's myth where the others are men's myths: i.e. the Pagan stories are God expressing Himself through the minds of poets, using such images as He found there, while Christianity is God expressing Himself through what we call "real things."[5]

This is a rather extraordinary conclusion for Lewis. Notice that he was able to simultaneously sustain a deep appreciation for pagan mythology—even describing it as a place where God is "expressing Himself"—while upholding the ultimate nature of the story of Christ. In Jesus, we see a "true myth," but it is different in one significant way: it "really happened."

Admittedly, no crisis is resolved in an instant: there are always precedents. Lewis had been set up for this conclusion by a stunning conversation with a cynical atheist colleague at Oxford, T. D. "Harry" Weldon, a hard-boiled rationalist who was a tutor and lecturer in greats (classical philosophy) at Magdalen College. That day in April 1926, Weldon grumbled about the historical veracity of the Gospels, particularly of Jesus's rising and dying, in light of other myths such as those James Frazer analyzed in his famous book *The Golden Bough*. Weldon groused, "All that stuff of Frazer's about the Dying God. Rum thing. It almost looks as if it had really happened once."[6] Of course, Weldon, who since that moment had never "showed any interest in Christianity," added the *almost*—it *almost* happened once. Lewis, as we know, arrived at a quite different conclusion.

But here is something noteworthy: on the one hand, Lewis's conclusion about Jesus implies that there are truly valuable elements in other religions and myths. On the other, it indicates the uniqueness and supremacy of Christ. Because these two emphases combine in Lewis, I will have to take them together. But first I would like to weave in my own experience with the crisis of the uniqueness of Jesus Christ.

MY STRUGGLE WITH
THE TRUTH OF OTHER RELIGIONS

To speak personally for a moment, as I read through journals from my late teen years, one of the first things that struck

me—besides the unbelievable emotional swings of late ado-
lescence—was my struggle with the uniqueness of Jesus. In
a section from January 1981, when I was grappling with the
Christian message about Jesus, there's an entry named "My
Belief in Religion: What Stops Me." It is a very sparse but
poignant entry: "So many religions." And then a bit later this:
"I'm having a lot of problems believing in Jesus Christ. It's so
narrowly defined."

These concerns are not in any way diminished today
for people seeking to understand Jesus. In fact, as a pastor
over the years to college students and post-college twenty-
somethings, I know that these concerns are tantamount for
people considering Christian faith and for those who are believers in Christ seeking to maintain the truth of their convictions.

And in 1981, I needed to know where Jesus fit. During
that decisive, life-altering winter quarter of my freshman year,
on the subject of the uniqueness of Jesus, Lewis came to me
as a mentor or perhaps, in Lewis's words, a teacher. (In *The
Great Divorce*, Lewis's great teacher, the pastor and fantasy
writer George MacDonald, accompanies him in the afterlife,
revealing that he has been there throughout Lewis's earthly
life. Lewis, it seems, may be my George MacDonald.) Lewis
helped me to understand the value of other religions and
myths but also to see that Jesus Christ is unique and worthy
of our worship.

FULFILLMENT MODEL

Lewis's view of the uniqueness of Christ was not that all other
faiths were entirely false but were brought to completion with
the revelation of Christ. I call it a *fulfillment model*—"Christ, in
transcending and thus abrogating, also fulfills, both Paganism
and Judaism."[7] Lewis, more generally, believes the Christian
story fulfills the hopes and directions of other religions, but in

stating this conviction, Lewis implies that the other religions, or myths, contain truth. He phrased the issue this way as he approached his own conversion to Christianity at age thirty-two—the task did not lie in finding one true religion among a thousand false ones. "It was rather, 'Where has religion reached its true maturity? Where, if anywhere, have the hints of all Paganism been fulfilled?' "[8] This approach struck me as reasonable then and still does. Why? We don't have to deny the truth and insight in other myths and different forms of thought, but we do hold fast to the gospel of mere Christianity—that Jesus is God incarnate. Lewis led me to resolve the problem of the uniqueness of Jesus in a secular and pluralistic world.

I think this offers the appropriate context for Lewis's "trilemma"—which he presents most famously in *Mere Christianity*—about whether Jesus is liar, Lord, or lunatic. Lewis argued that we do not have the luxury of calling him a "great moral teacher," and the first two options are nonsensical. Therefore Jesus is who the Gospels present him to be: the Son of God, the Lord. Here's how he phrased it in *The Problem of Pain*:

> There was a man born among these Jews who claimed to be, or to be the son of, or to be "one with," the Something which is at once the awful haunter of nature [a form of Lewis's second apologetic argument] and the giver of the moral law [third apologetic]. . . . Either he was a raving lunatic of an unusually abominable type, or else He was, and is, precisely what He said. There is no middle way.[9]

And then later, in the BBC Broadcast talks that eventually became published as *Mere Christianity*, instead of simply presenting a dilemma—Jesus is a lunatic or else "what He said," the argument presents three options, a "trilemma" (and these might be some of the most famous sentences Lewis ever wrote):

> A man who was merely a man and said the sort of things Jesus said would not be a great moral teacher. He would

either be a lunatic—on the level with a man who says he is a poached egg—or he would be the devil of hell. You must take your choice. Either this was, and is, the Son of God, or else a madman or something worse. You can shut Him up for a fool . . . or you can fall at His feet and call Him Lord and God. But let us not come with any patronizing nonsense about His being a great human teacher. He has not left that open to us.[10]

Lewis wants to disturb us from any easy middle ground with Jesus as a "good teacher." As he writes in *Miracles*, we cannot bring together the *"shrewdness* of His moral teaching and the rampant megalomania"[11] without Jesus Christ's divinity. With his trilemma, Lewis pushes us to a decision. And yet to any reader sensitive to the complexities of responding to Jesus, let alone the problems of resolving easily what He said in the Gospels, this argument appears to be a bit hasty or at least rather lapidary. How can he expect to resolve Christ's uniqueness in one paragraph? I'm not certain that Lewis had an immense amount of interest in the complexities, but he does elaborate his thinking in an essay that appeared later in the collection assembled as *God in the Dock* titled, "What Are We to Make of Jesus Christ?"[12] Lewis presents several key points: First of all, that Jesus forgives sins—not simply offenses against him, but all sins. Jesus says, "before Abraham was, I am" (John 8:58) and a host of other statements that would characterize him as a megalomaniac. Nonetheless, his moral teachings are sane and humble. Lewis asks, Would his first followers have exaggerated his claims? As Jews, they were the least likely to do so because they believed in the one God. If the claims were exaggerated, they would have to come in the form of legend. But in the Gospels, there is realism, like Christ scribbling in the sand in John 8:6–8, that does not correspond to the form of literature known as legend. It can only be compared to twentieth-century novels: "the art of *inventing* little irrelevant details to make an imaginary scene more convincing is a purely modern art."[13] Above all, there is the resurrection, which is not simply the hope of survival, but something the New Testament writers present as entirely new and earth-shattering. Who would create this claim?

Lewis returns to this trilemma in the first and last installments of his famous The Chronicles of Narnia series. As so often happens, he worked out major ideas in both nonfiction and fiction. In *The Lion, the Witch, and the Wardrobe* Lucy and Edmund have both discovered Narnia through the wardrobe door, but Edmund (who is trying to hide the fact that he has met the White Witch, Jadis) denies the experience and asserts that Lucy is lying. The next morning, Peter and Susan approach the Professor. They are convinced that he will immediately contact their parents when Lucy tells her story. He invites the children into his study and listens to their story from beginning to end without interrupting. When they are finished, to their surprise, the Professor asks them why they are so certain that Lucy's story isn't true. He asks them to consider their own past experiences with Lucy and Edmund. Who, he asks, is more truthful? He then admonishes them to use logic, lamenting, "Why don't they teach logic at these schools?" Logically—and here's the key—the Professor concludes that Lucy is either telling lies, going mad, or telling the truth. Since Lucy is not a liar and is not going mad, she must therefore be telling the truth.[14] The analogy is reasonably clear: if Lucy is generally trustworthy, then her testimony about another world— even if it contradicts materialist assumptions—can be trusted. Accordingly, the witnesses to Jesus's unique status as the Son of God are credible witnesses to what they tell us, even if it seems absurd.

Materialism may lead us to implicitly reject the conclusion that Jesus Christ is Lord, but it may also sound exclusivist, narrow, parochial, and frankly impossible in a world where so many call on other names of other gods or may have never heard the name Jesus. In that light, a few pages after presenting the trilemma in *Mere Christianity*, Lewis offers this clarification: "We do know that no man can be saved except through Christ; we do not know that only those who know Him can be saved through Him."[15]

How do we best understand Lewis's Christology? In this fulfillment paradigm for Christ, Lewis brings together his uniqueness with an appreciation for other myths, and I find this a bit stunning, especially since he sounds a great deal like the twentieth-century Swiss theologian Karl Barth. This is a surprise because Lewis said some tart words about Barth, once writing to his brother that Oxford students were "reading a dreadful man called Karl Barth."[16] Still he seems never to have read Barth directly. "Barth I have never read, or not that I remember."[17] It would have benefited Lewis to read Barth because he, like Lewis (to lean on George Hunsinger's phrasing), presented *exclusivism without triumphalism* or, alternatively, *inclusivism without compromise.*" In other words, they both believe in one theological scheme representing the truth—I would offer instead, one person—but other schemes (and for Lewis, these take the form of myths) are not entirely mistaken and even provide glimpses of truth.[18]

Similarly, there can be salvation for those who don't necessarily name Jesus. As he wrote to Mrs. Johnson,

> I think that every prayer which is sincerely made even to a false god or to a v. imperfectly conceived true God, is accepted by the true God and that Christ saves many who do not think they know Him. For He is (dimly) present in the *good* side of the inferior teachers they follow. In the parable of the Sheep & Goats (Matt. XXV.31 and following) those who are saved do not seem to know that they have served Christ.[19]

He also portrayed this conviction in *The Last Battle,* where the character of Emeth embodies this other side: that those who don't hear about Jesus in life can be saved. Put another way, there is salvation outside of the church. (This has been a famous theological question through the ages: "Is there salvation outside the walls of the church?" In other words, salvation for those who haven't heard.) Emeth (whose name means "truth" in Hebrew) has been a Calormene prince who has never served Aslan but who instead serves the god of his country, Tash. When he dies, he's surprised to find that Aslan greets him in the life to come with allusions to Jeremiah 29:13 and Matthew 7:7: "All the service thou hast done to Tash, I account as service done to me. . . . *For all find what they truly seek.*"[20]

EVALUATION

My overall contention in this book is that Lewis has something to say not simply to mid-twentieth-century Christians but to contemporary Christians well. How, then, do I evaluate Lewis's fulfillment model of Jesus in a world of pluralism? How well does the "liar, Lord, lunatic" argument work today?

I'll begin with some concerns.

His "liar, Lord, or lunatic" argument needs further engagement with other noncanonical gospels, especially those popularized by books such as the bestseller of all time, *The Da Vinci Code*. These noncanonical sources have only gained in acclaim since his death. In my opinion, many of them are so late and tainted by gnostic thought that they are not historically useful, at least not useful in understanding the historical Jesus of Nazareth. Nevertheless, in some there is some strong historical tradition, such as that embedded within the *Gospel of Thomas*. Although I realize this topic engenders considerable debate today, historically the most secure documents for finding out about Jesus are the biblical Gospels.[21] And yet, Lewis's argument would have been stronger had he engaged more thoroughly with these sources.

The contemporary reader probably also brings a higher degree of skepticism about the Christian church. Lewis does not spend much time on the uniqueness of the Christian church, which remains a key issue today for those outside the church. Or perhaps better formulated, Lewis sees a fairly direct line of continuity between believing in Jesus and the community of believers in Jesus as the church. We will see in the next chapter that the authority of the Bible depends, for Lewis, on the testimony of the Christian community or the church. Certainly, as he famously wrote, he promoted "mere Christianity," not any particular denomination. Still, for many there is no direct line from belief in Jesus as the Son of God to belief in the church, but the church's witness—and its veracity—is critical to judging the Gospels as reliable.

In some ways, it would be nicer to soften the Gospels' claim of the unique status of Jesus. As much as that would make our lives easier, the emphasis of the Bible and the confessions of Christianity over time state that something singular happened in Jesus. Ultimately there is no other God than the one revealed in Jesus Christ. I realize that this may be an "opening bid" in the conversation with non-Christians that closes down the conversation, but that fact is simply the "stumbling block" of the gospel that Paul writes about in 1 Corinthians 1:23.

I hope the reader will allow me one last, idiosyncratic issue. At first I couldn't grasp how Jesus's death makes a positive difference for us. Even if Christ is Lord, what difference does that make for us? Lewis had difficulties here too. After becoming a Christian, Lewis could not easily subscribe to the notion that Christ substituted himself for us. "What I couldn't see was how the life and death of Someone Else (whoever he was) 2000 years ago could help us here and now—except in so far as his *example* helped us."[22] Though I've come to appreciate the substitutionary death better over the subsequent years, I still find resonance in Lewis's conclusion that he drew a little over a decade after his conversion. In effect, theories about Christ's atonement are not the final issue. Historically, in fact, Lewis is in good company with the church historically. Though it has defined who Christ is—or Christology—there has been no ecumenical statement on atonement.

> We are told that Christ was killed for us, that His death has washed out our sins, and that by dying He disabled death itself. That is the formula. That is Christianity. . . . Any theories we build up as to how Christ's death did all this are, in my view, quite secondary: mere plans or diagrams to be left alone if they do not help us, and, even if they do help us, not to be confused with the thing itself.[23]

More positively and speaking biographically, Lewis led me to see that the witness to Jesus in the Gospels demands that I respond. He is "either God or a bad man." Put simply, through the Gospels, I found that Jesus demands a response and that his truth—ultimate though it is—does not invalidate other insights. Instead it is "the true Light, which lighteth every man," as John 1:9 puts it. I think this is why this apologetic argument has power. It puts the listener right at the heart of the Christian faith. Lewis doesn't just stop with a generalized god of theism but asks us, What are you going to do about Jesus Christ? That indeed was the question posed to him, and that is the crisis he sets us in. That is the crisis he wants to help us resolve by finding that Jesus is Lord.

But Lewis also intrigues me because he offers a model that finds truth in myths. Here I expand this to other philosophies, religious traditions, cultures, etc. I have particularly pursued this method with the dialogue of theology and science, but that's simply one option. This aspect of Lewis's fourth apologetic step is equally powerful and closer to the crisis Lewis faced. Over burgers and a brew I talked one pleasant Chico afternoon with a brilliant grad student, Matthew, who told me that this particular argument of Lewis brought him back to faith. Matthew read in *Miracles* that God's light could shine through myths (like that of the Corn King, Adonis, etc.). While serving in the war in Iraq, he told me, "tears streamed down my face." Lewis provided a needed resolution to a significant crisis he faced with Christian belief.

And this brings me to final point on Lewis's fulfillment model that cuts both ways. If one were simply to read *Mere Christianity*, it might sound like the acceptance of Jesus as the Son of God is the only rational decision. But many people I know simply don't agree. The very fact is that most of those who heard Jesus's message did not become members of the growing Christian church. Besides intellectual problems—like the questions about the truth of the Gospels and what they really declare about Jesus—to say yes to the gospel is to be ready to turn around. Here Lewis has not clarified sufficiently that this decision for Christ as the Son of God is self-involving. This I learned from both N. T. Wright and Blaise Pascal, but also from my own experience. Lewis knew this too. In conversion, God interferes with our lives. We relinquish autonomy. If we find the gospel message to be true, we need to surrender to God and change our lives. For that reason—whether or not the trilemma or some form of it works—many will still never assent that Jesus is God.

CONCLUSION

In sum, we've seen that Lewis believed that many myths pointed to God's truth but that in Christ myth becomes fact, and therefore we have to deal with his claims and whether they make him a liar, Lord, or lunatic. It's important to see where this trilemma fits in Lewis. He isn't arguing for a triumphalistic, narrowly defined argument about Christ's supremacy. Instead he argues that God is already speaking through other religions and myths but has spoken uniquely and definitively in Jesus. This conclusion rounds out the final component of his four-step apologetic.

Lewis's conclusions about Christ also imply that we have to rely on the main and most historically secure documents, the New Testament. That brings us to the question and the second key problem for contemporary Christians: How can we believe in a two-thousand-year-old set of writings, especially the first-century Gospels that specifically present Jesus? And what exactly did C. S. Lewis believe about the Bible? How could this brilliant Oxford literary scholar believe in this book above all others? That is the subject of the next chapter.

Chapter 6

THE CRISIS OF THE BIBLE

I have been suspected of being what is called a Fundamentalist.

Lewis, *Reflections on the Psalms*

I BEGIN THIS CHAPTER WITH A DISCLAIMER: CLIVE STAPLES LEWIS was not an American evangelical. For one thing, he wasn't from the United States, but Ireland, even if the bulk of his readership is American. (And this fact deserves a parenthesis: When I visited Oxford in doing research for this book, I was surprised to note how much attention J. R. R. Tolkien—and particularly The Lord of the Rings—received, while praise for Lewis was more muted. I suspect the latter's vocal Christian faith remains the culprit. All this is to say that his reception in England is not as enthusiastic as it is in the States.) More importantly, as a member of the Church of England, Lewis was, as he describes it, "not especially 'high,' nor especially 'low,' nor especially anything else."[1] Thus, at least in a nominal sense, he was no evangelical.

And yet his reception in the United States has been most conspicuously evangelical (even if many outside evangelicalism love The Chronicles of Narnia in book and movie form).

Perhaps this fact arose from many of his literary papers going not only to Oxford but also to the evangelical bastion Wheaton College, which produced Billy Graham, Philip Yancey, and Carl Henry. It's also Lewis's commitment to theological realism (the belief that God really does exist) and his general orthodoxy that heartens evangelicals. Still, what I have discovered in returning to Lewis—as someone who has been nurtured both by mainline and evangelical Protestant theology and who cares most passionately about "mere Christianity"— is that he offers surprises to party-line evangelicals, particularly in his views of Scripture and other religions.

There is another side to this issue: some people back away from Lewis because he's associated with evangelicalism, and this leads to a different type of crisis for Lewis: his work is meant to speak to the universal church. He wanted to speak not from a faction of the church but about "mere Christianity." Nonetheless—and because of Lewis's evangelical reception— I have met many over the past few years who did not want to read Lewis because of his alleged "fundamentalist" views. So in this chapter and the next I'll try to undo this misconception, and I believe this chapter will surprise many readers who only know *about* Lewis but have not read his work directly.

Lewis did not have a conservative evangelical's crisis with the Bible. Despite accusations of being a fundamentalist, he wasn't an inerrantist who would become overwrought about whether Satan commanded David to take a census of Israel (as in 1 Chr. 21:1) or God did (as in 2 Sam. 24:1). He did not particularly seem to care if there was an angel at Jesus's tomb (Matt.) or if it was a young man (Mark). Lewis doesn't really fit into evangelicalism, and it's worth noting that some evangelical gatekeepers become especially nervous about his understanding of Scripture. A fairly cursory jaunt through the Internet unveils several self-described evangelical commentators disappointed by Lewis's view on Scripture. They demand a commitment to the Bible's inerrancy and its literal interpretation, and so they are quite happy to jettison Lewis from their theological camp, even to the point of denying his place in heaven.[2]

Clearly fundamentalists would not count him as one of theirs. The very notion that being labeled as such is a slur comes from those who think it's not at all a badge of honor. The quip comes from those who find it silly that he believed the Bible at all. It's a quip that points out the crisis that Lewis was trying to overcome—not from the position of literalists and inerrantists but from the liberal angle that it's all myth anyway. And "myth" in this case means "fiction," as I've outlined in the previous chapter. So to grasp Lewis and his relationship with Scripture, it's critically important to remember that Lewis's great resolution of the crisis of the nature of Jesus was that myth became fact. In other words, he did not resist the importance of myth—that was already active. The question that presented a crisis to Lewis is this: How can Jesus Christ stand out against other myths? Similarly, how can the Bible have unique authority among all other books?

Simply reading the Bible didn't resolve Lewis's problems. When Lewis originally read the Bible in his adult life, as he first began to take on Christian faith, he struggled with its meaning. Just after his conversion to Christianity, he wrote to his long-time friend, Arthur Greeves, "I have just finished *The Epistle to the Romans*, the first Pauline epistle I have ever seriously thought about. It contains many difficult and some horrible things."[3] Let's not miss it: he says not simply "difficult" but also "horrible." This tussle with the Holy Book continued. Even late in life, and although he read the Bible daily, when he reflected on Scripture in his late fifties, he continued to wonder about Paul: "I cannot be the only reader who has wondered why God, having given him so many gifts, withheld from him (what would to us seem so necessary for the first Christian theologian) that of lucidity and orderly exposition."[4] So Lewis's encounter with Scripture reveals a crisis for him: How does this book, with its flaws and problems, still carry God's word to us?

To answer that question, I will focus on four major themes in this chapter: first of all, Lewis believed that the Bible has authority because of the church's ongoing historical testimony and the power of the one Word, Jesus Christ; second, that human flaws shone through the pages of the Bible and yet it carries the Word of God; third, that its mythical character does not imply that the Bible is fictional; and most importantly, that Christian lives are formed by reading the Bible.

THE AUTHORITY OF THE BIBLE

First of all, Lewis could not believe in the authority of the Bible because of its unimpeachable style. Instead Lewis realized that believing in this book above all the other books that he loved required an outside source of authority. First of all, he trusted in the truth of Scripture because of the witness of the church. This quote from his first sustained nonfiction apologetic, *The Problem of Pain*, discloses Lewis's willingness not to have a perfect, inerrant Bible, his love of myth, and his respect for the tradition of the church. He is discussing the Genesis 3 story of the fall of humankind:

> I have the deepest respect even for Pagan myths, still more for myths in Holy Scripture. . . . I assume the Holy Spirit would not have allowed the latter to grow up in the Church and win the assent of great doctors unless it also was true and useful as far as it went.[5]

The church, as the deposit of ongoing testimony, affirms the Bible's truth and validity.

Secondly, Lewis's approach to the crisis of the Bible is in fact closely tied to his resolution of the crisis of Jesus. As Jesus is the unique Lord, his character gives clarity to the character of the Scriptures as carrying God's Word. For that reason we gain the most clarity in understanding the Bible by keeping in mind Lewis's view on Jesus. Myth was critical for understanding Christ; it is critical for grasping Lewis's views on the Bible. I will have more to say on this below.

THE BIBLE HAS FLAWS
BUT CARRIES THE WORD OF GOD

What exactly was Lewis's understanding of Scripture? Here the reader clearly realizes that Lewis was not a systematic theologian. There is no elaborated doctrine of Holy Scripture in his corpus. In fact, his views on Scripture are living and literary, and thus a doctrinal approach is what we should not expect. Instead, we find that Lewis is free to offer occasional comments as they relate to other topics he is addressing. In a letter written close to this time, he responded to Janet Wise, who regarded herself as being "an *intelligent* Fundamentalist," with these words:

> My own position is not Fundamentalist, if Fundamentalism means accepting as a point of faith at the outset the proposition 'Every statement in the Bible is completely true in the literal historical sense.' That wd. [would] break down at once on the parables."[6]

By this statement, Lewis means that he does not believe in the necessity of inerrancy and historical facticity in all its parts (more on that below) for the Bible to be true. In his 1958 *Reflections on the Psalms*, in a chapter simply titled "Scripture," Lewis comes closest to a systematic statement on the Bible. He lays out how the Bible carries the Word of God. Lewis clearly outlines Scripture's human frailties.

> The human qualities of the raw materials show through. Naivety, error, contradiction, even (as in the cursing Psalms)

wickedness are not removed. The total result is not "the Word of God" in the sense that every passage, in itself, gives impeccable science or history. It carries the Word of God; and we (under grace, with attention to tradition and to interpreters wiser than ourselves, and with the use of such intelligence and learning as we may have) receive that word from it not by using it as an encyclopedia or an encyclical but by steeping ourselves in its tone or temper and so learning its overall message.[7]

"It carries the Word of God," and this implies that the Bible is not itself identical with the word: "It is Christ Himself, not the Bible, who is the true word of God. The Bible, read in the right spirit and with the guidance of good teachers, will bring us to him."[8] So the authority of the Bible, as I noted above, derives from Christ. It is, in this sense, a borrowed authority. For that reason, we learn the truth of Scripture by focusing on Christ, the Word. To follow Lewis, we must not make the Bible the fourth member of the Trinity.

"It carries the Word of God." This phrase exemplifies Lewis's view of Scripture. In some level of tension with carrying the divine Word, there is humanness: "naivety, error, contradiction, even... wickedness." These are words that make conservative evangelical Christians—and especially Fundamentalists—cringe. Some even respond venomously when they read Lewis's understanding of Scripture. Lewis is willing to concede that the Bible is not flawless. In fact, Lewis is closer to a mainline, sometimes called "neo-orthodox," perspective. Many of his insights mirror Barth's approach. The authority of the Bible as a witness that "carries the Word of God" ultimately derives from Jesus Christ as the one Word of God.[9] The flaws in the Scripture do not invalidate that it is also a way that God speaks in self-revelation.

If this presents a problem for some readers of Scripture, it didn't for Lewis. Why? He loved myth. How extreme was that love? In his first years at Oxford, he learned the Icelandic language so he could join Tolkien's Kolbiter's club to study the myths of "northerness." Both he and Tolkien had a high regard for myth. But how did this lover of myth define it? So often, we hear "myth" set against what is historical or what is true. First of all, Lewis would have agreed that myth often relates what is not historical, except, crucially, when myth became fact in Jesus.

Understanding Lewis's definition of myth is critical because his view of Scripture as myth resolved most of his difficulties with the Bible. For Lewis, a myth is not made up or untrue. It is "at its best, a real unfocused gleam of divine truth falling on human imagination."[10] A myth, like a parable, therefore gives us truth through narrative or story. As Lewis wrote, "What flows into you from the myth is not truth but reality (truth is always *about* something, but reality is that *about which* truth is)."[11] Instead of "myth," I would use the term "meaningful story," and, as a generation schooled on the stories in film, we should not have any difficulty grasping this.

Therefore, myth, for Lewis, communicates God's reality. The Bible's message can be conveyed through nonhistorical stories. Lewis appears to have been reluctant to make this statement too publicly; indeed, in one of his clearest earlier expressions, a May 4, 1953, letter to Corbin Carnell, he writes, "I am myself a little uneasy about the question you raise" about the Bible's historicity. But he continues by writing that Jonah does not need to be read as history in the same way the accounts of David's court or the New Testament accounts do because Jonah "has to me the air of being a moral romance."[12] In a May 7, 1959, letter to Clyde Kilby, Lewis ruled out "the view that inspiration is the single thing in the sense that, if present at all, it is always present in the same mode and the same degree" by noting such features as the discrepancies in the genealogies of Matthew 1 and Luke 3, the different death accounts of Judas in Matthew 27 and Acts 1, and the unhistoricity of the parables and probably Jonah and Job, among other things.[13]

So there are places where the Bible can be mythical—and thus fictional—and true in a sense that pure proposition or historical recounting could never be. But Lewis would not conclude that all portions of the Bible are mythical and therefore unhistorical.

MYTH DOESN'T ALWAYS MEAN FICTIONAL

The context for Lewis's essay "Modern Theology and Biblical Criticism"[14] explains a great deal because it demonstrates that even though Lewis appreciated the existence of myth in the Bible, he did not mean that it is therefore always unhistorical. Lewis was goaded by a comment from theologian Alec Vidler that the miracle of turning water into wine was actually a parable. After a dinner and some sherry with Kenneth Carey, the Principal of Westcott House, Cambridge, Lewis commented that "it was quite incredible that we should have to wait 2000 years to be told by a theologian called Vidler what the Church has always regarded as a miracle was, in fact, a parable!"[15] In that light, Dr. Carey invited Lewis to present his ideas, which he subsequently did.

Put simply, this essay exemplifies two key concerns: the Bible is historical when it presents itself as such, and miracles do not invalidate the Bible's claim to factual history. As a result, we cannot rule out miracles in advance. This little essay (and lecture) offers a clear insight into what Lewis held fast to—that miracles cannot be excluded from the Gospels a priori and that in Jesus "myth became fact." Or put another way, the Gospels present real history.

Important here is that Lewis is taking on a major tenet of twentieth-century biblical criticism. The legendary and erudite scholar Rudolf Bultmann's call to "demythologize" the New Testament has certainly faded in the past fifty years or so, but in the middle of the twentieth century, it was arguably *the* concern of New Testament scholarship. Not only that, but Lewis is on sure academic footing with Bultmann; with Lewis's extensive training in literature, his subsequent teaching in the field of classics, and his constant reading of those texts, it's not an exaggeration to say that Lewis had more experience with actually reading myths than this leading advocate of "demythologizing." So when he asks what is so wrong with myth, it strikes at the core question. Many readers of the Bible today would shrug their shoulders and reply, "Nothing's wrong with myth." More recently, biblical criticism has emphasized narrative theology and thus the story of the Bible, which is another way of addressing mythic elements.

Finally, to say that the Bible's mythological elements do not mean it is fiction, Lewis takes his considerable reading of fiction to the topic. And here he outshines Bultmann, who, like many biblical critics, reads the Bible in a fairly wooden way. This I also learned when I studied biblical criticism after completing a degree in comparative literature. Few of my professors—excellent as they were in many ways with Greek exegesis, analysis of inter-textual questions, and the history surrounding the New Testament—really grasped Lewis's essential point as they sliced the Gospel records into what is history and what is tradition: the New Testament is not artful enough to be fiction.

At the time of my first reading of the Gospels when I was assessing whether the portrayal of Jesus was historically reliable and thus whether he was truly worthy of our devotion, my best tools for interpreting these narratives were my budding skills as a student of comparative literature. I soon realized that Jesus, this central figure of the Gospels, wasn't some fictional protagonist. Mark, for example, writes his Gospel in very rough language. The Gospels include details that don't necessarily carry the story along but have the hard authenticity of history—the man who runs away naked in Mark's Gospel when confronted by the soldiers, or the one hundred fifty-three fish that the disciples catch at the end of the Gospel of John. I realize today—after some years in seminary—that each writer of the Gospels and Epistles has a particular angle on Jesus, and I'm more sensitive to this variety. Nonetheless, a *person* comes through: Jesus's personality and actions never appear to me as modeled by my expectations; instead they keep pushing back against my preconceptions. His utterances display the insistent character of truth.

All this brings me to say that Lewis's literary approach to Scripture, his ability to sort out history from fiction, and his appreciation of myth (or story) spoke to my crisis with, or at least questions about, the Bible. It provided me with a way to be formed by Scripture.

WE LEARN HOW TO READ
THE BIBLE BY BEING FORMED BY IT

"There is nothing in literature," Lewis wrote in his first famous academic study, *The Allegory of Love*, "which does not, in some degree, percolate into life."[16] If that is accurate for literature as a whole, how much more so for Holy Scripture. When we read Scripture, we become what God wants for us.

I return again to Lewis's quote on Scripture from *Reflections on the Psalms* stating that we must use the Bible "by steeping ourselves in its tone and temper and so learning its overall message"[17]—we are required to read so that we truly grasp the full character of the Bible. We enter its "strange new world," to quote Barth again.[18] This is not a mathematical table that we can memorize; it is a living document with a vibrant history. Accordingly, Lewis is not willing to equate the exact words of the Bible with God's very speech. Instead, "by steeping ourselves in the tone and temper," we make ourselves able to grasp the meaning of Scripture and thus learn its overall message. Lewis here defends and promotes the reading of literature for what it says, *not* for some theory *about it.*

Another angle on Lewis's concerns about Scripture is that he wanted his readers to find Christianity itself, not finding himself convinced by the various attempts at speculating on the "historical Jesus" that emerged every year. (A trend that has accelerated since his time.) Lewis was convinced that we must be careful of creating a new Jesus every year. As he puts into the mouth of the demonic tempter Screwtape, first the historical Jesus is promoted on liberal and humanitarian lines, and next it is featured on Marxian ones.[19]

> The advantages of these constructions, which we intend to change every thirty years or so, are manifold. In the first place they all tend to direct men's devotion to something which does not exist, for each "historical Jesus" is unhistorical.[20]

The problem here is that we, as readers of the Bible, would learn to read *about* other people's views of Jesus, not Jesus's own words. So Screwtape continues; the documents remain what they are, so each new historical Jesus has to suppress some points and emphasize others—"*brilliant* is the adjective we teach humans to apply to it." We then arrive at Lewis's primary concern: Screwtape wants to destroy devotional life. Instead of "the real presence of the Enemy . . . we substitute a merely probable, remote, shadowy, and uncouth figure, one who spoke a strange language and died a long time ago. Such an object cannot in fact be worshipped."[21]

Now if Lewis believed that Satan's plan was to remove our ability to devote ourselves to Christ by creating new Jesuses, he instead encouraged us to focus on what actually took place in Christ. Therefore we understand the Bible best by looking at the Incarnation. In his preface to J. B. Phillips's translation of the New Testament, he defends the propriety of updating the language of the Scripture beyond the 1611 version of the King James. He comments on the *koine*, or "common" Greek of the New Testament: "The New Testament in the original Greek is not a work of literary art: it is not written in a solemn, ecclesiastical language." It employs "a sort of 'basic' Greek; a language without roots in the soil, a utilitarian, commercial and administrative language."[22] Lewis's clarity in grasping the character of the language of the New Testament grabs my attention. (As a New Testament professor once commented about the Greek of the Second Gospel: "Mark writes like a fourth grader.") But even more worthy of note is how he draws an inference between the biblical language and the Incarnation of Christ:

> Does this shock us? It ought not to, except as the Incarnation itself ought to shock us. The same divine humility which decreed that God should become a baby at a peasant-woman's breast, and later an arrested field-preacher in the hands of the Roman police, decreed also that He should be preached in a vulgar, prosaic and unliterary language. If you can stomach the one, you can stomach the other. The Incarnation is in that sense an irreverent doctrine: Christianity, in that sense, an incurably irreverent religion.[23]

Lewis believes that we might maintain the wrong kind of "reverence" in God's coming to earth as a human being; similarly the Bible's form is common and vulgar—in this sense meaning the common language of the peasant, not the exalted language of the trained scholar. God is a shocking God indeed, who enters into real life. The roughness of the Bible is a clue to recognizing this irreverent God.

EVALUATION

I have always appreciated when C. S. Lewis, a truly world-class literary scholar, commented on the Holy Book. If one-tenth of contemporary biblical scholars possessed his literary sensitivity, there would be a higher standard level of biblical scholarship today. We do have to take him seriously when he confessed that he was not a biblical scholar. He wasn't. We have to do more than simply look at textual criticism, as he asserts in "Modern Theology and Biblical Criticism."[24] We must, for example, employ redaction and source criticism. In addition, the nature of his occasional remarks on the Bible leave us wanting more, something comprehensive and systematic. We need a clearer statement on why we should believe the Bible: How do we know what comments are true or false? If some reveal wickedness, then which ones reveal holiness, and why? He may not have needed to respond to every question about the Bible, but we cannot remain content with Lewis alone as our guide.

Does Lewis help us today, especially in light of science? Many impugn the Bible's truth because it doesn't match with the advance of scientific knowledge. It seems outdated and surpassed. In response, it's crucial to recall that Lewis never believed that science—nor what he called "the Scientific Outlook," which I outlined in chapter 2—should be the final arbiter of truth. So he forcefully and consistently argued against science and its norms standing above other forms of knowledge and authorities, such as the ongoing testimony of the church in the case of the Bible. This means that his understanding of Scripture leads to a model of independence in its relationship with science. This approach may at times help Christians avoid pseudo-problems with the Bible when it does not provide, in his words, "impeccable science."[25] For example, Lewis writes, Genesis 1–2 probably "derived from earlier Semitic stories which were Pagan and mythical,"[26] and yet under the guidance of the Father of lights, it became a vehicle for the profound and true story of creation. All this implies no need to justify the truth of these texts against the modern science of Big Bang cosmology or evolution. It may, however, also leave some wanting more connection with the obvious power and insights of science.

The final truth of Scripture lies elsewhere. Lewis believed that we must be formed by Holy Scripture—his best point, in my opinion. According to *The C. S. Lewis Bible,* Lewis read the Bible every day.[27] He sought God in the pages of Scripture. As a professor of literature, he taught so his students would know about the books they read, not about theories about the books they read; similarly he would be most disturbed by any theories that obscure the key message of the Bible, Jesus Christ. He desired that we are formed by reading Scripture, not by reading *about* or talking *about* it. For Lewis, more than a theory about Scripture, the key is practicing its truths. Or better, it is only when we are formed by the Bible, when we are steeped in Jesus's teaching, that our hearts with no "less fine of mesh than love . . . will hold the sacred Fish."[28] To those of us who hold to "Scripture alone" (as I do) as the way to find God and to form our lives (what the Reformation called *sola scriptura*), Lewis's words are good indeed.

I now turn to Lewis's words for those who have not turned the pages of Scripture as I look at the ways he addressed the crises common to all human beings. Naturally, these two categories—those crises specific to Christians and those that apply to all humankind—are not airtight. And, when Lewis looks at any topic, he does so from his convictions as a follower of Christ. Nevertheless, there is no one on this planet who has evaded the crises of feeling, of suffering, and of death.

The Crises of Human Life

Chapter 7

THE CRISIS OF FEELING

Heed not thy feelings: Do thy work.

George MacDonald

DURING THE EARLY 1960S, THE *CHRISTIAN CENTURY* PUBLISHED a series of answers by prominent authors to the question, "What books did most to shape your vocational attitude and your philosophy of life?" The June 6, 1962, issue featured C. S. Lewis. Here are the ten books in his list:

1. *Phantastes* by George MacDonald
2. *The Everlasting Man* by G. K. Chesterton
3. *The Aeneid* by Virgil
4. *The Temple* by George Herbert
5. *The Prelude* by William Wordsworth
6. *The Idea of the Holy* by Rudolf Otto
7. *The Consolation of Philosophy* by Boethius
8. *Life of Samuel Johnson* by James Boswell
9. *Descent into Hell* by Charles Williams
10. *Theism and Humanism* by Arthur James Balfour

What strikes me is the mixture. Some have a specific engagement with secular philosophy—here I particularly highlight Boethius's sixth-century *Consolation* and his profound critical reception of Greek philosophy. Others are especially Christian, like Chesterton's *Everlasting Man*, which offers a Christian vision of all human history and which affected Lewis profoundly; similarly affecting was MacDonald's *Phantastes*, a book that Lewis said baptized his teenage imagination. He read both before he became a Christian—one provided a rational vision, a supposition of how to make sense of history from Christian faith; the other featured an imaginative approach to Christian truth. But others are not in any way Christian, like *The Aeneid*, written decades before Christ and which Lewis loved so much he began a translation of this classic. This too moved and shaped him.

Since Lewis was foremost a literary man, this list also reveals a great deal about three sides of Lewis and mirrors the three sets of crises I am analyzing: first of all, those related to moving away from atheism; second, those that had a theological focus; and finally, those that expressed common human themes. Indeed, to this point, I have looked at Lewis's crises with atheism: the reasons that not believing in God became problematic and how he leveraged those insights to create a powerful set of apologetics. Outside of his fantasy work in The Chronicles of Narnia (where some of this apologetic work is slipped in through imagination), Lewis is perhaps best known for countering atheism. I have also explored how he turned his considerable intellectual and imaginative powers to the crises of Christian faith in the twentieth century and the issues presented by believing in Jesus Christ as the unique Son of God—even as this insight overlaps with his arguments against atheism—and then to the Bible as God's word. But there remains one additional side to him.

Lewis always maintained a healthy and sustained understanding of life as it is lived by all human beings: marked by disappointment and depression, suffering and trials, as well as the prospect of death, which we can all see and which none of us will escape. I suspect his setting in life—his teaching at two secular universities, Oxford and Cambridge—kept him mindful of those who never walked inside Magdalen College's chapel or read the pages of the King James Bible as a devotional practice.

Here was a man who relished a good walk, a pint of beer with his friends, and reading exceptional books. Here was a man who also described personal crises not limited to believers in Christ, like sorrow over the death of a friend in battle and disappointment over never achieving recognition as a poet. Indeed, the Bible itself recognizes the destiny of all humankind and its sorrows: "Yet man is born unto trouble, as the sparks fly upward" (Job 5:7). For this reason, I continue to turn to Lewis because, frankly, I'm not always drawn to people who display their spirituality too boldly in their writing or who seem to think that all of life consists of praying, reading Scripture, and singing hymns. Writers who resonate with me acknowledge the mundane things of life, like filling the car with gas; having keys copied at the hardware store; and buying butter, flour, and orange juice at the grocery store. They also acknowledge the hard things in life, like watching your children grow up, realizing your time on earth is also passing, seeing parents age and die, or grasping that dreams you once held will never come to pass.

FEELINGS ARE SECONDARY

Given all these daily, quotidian issues, how do we know what to do? Contemporary American culture has a nearly universal slogan: "If it feels right, do it." Feelings—particularly the emotional rush of life—remain the final arbiter of truth and decision making for our culture. And sadly that is true for those inside the church as well, where I often hear distrust of "head knowledge" and an emphasis on the interior life, which in this case usually means our emotions. Most of us would agree that, because it touches the desires of the heart, faith means more than intellectual assent to a group of fact. Yet with the way most of us define "heart" as a place where we feel emotion, this can come to mean that feelings are more important than thought.

Certainly it is the nature of American revivalism that we tend to want a "burning in the bosom" and the feeling of conversion. Too much of Christian spirituality implores us to introspection and seeing how the Lord is working and whether you feel God's joy. There are some historical roots: early Puritans, who were anxious about whether God had elected them or not, worried about signs of salvation, about whether they felt God's concerns, although this was never the response John Calvin wanted to the doctrine of predestination. Later in our history, revivalism looked to the "warming of the heart" as a sign of salvation—which is certainly an element of Christian belief—but often excluded rationality and obedience. Contemporarily, our obsession with feeling good has us wandering around in search of giddiness.

So this fixation on feelings is not new to the Christian faith, and even as this country has become less Christianized, we are still obsessed with feelings. But we should know better. Lewis certainly did. He was convinced that our feelings often deceive and that true life begins when the rush of feelings lets off. As he wrote in a letter from 1950, "Obedience is the key to all doors: *feelings* come (or don't come) and go as God pleases. We can't produce them at will and mustn't try."[1]

As I've emphasized above, Lewis was not given over simply to intellectual abstraction either. He believed that what we know must affect our lives. In this way, he mirrors the biblical emphasis on the heart not as the arbiter of emotions but as the center of action. So it's neither feelings nor abstract cognition that matters. Eugene Peterson, when he paraphrases the Bible in *The Message,* gets it exactly right in his rendering of Galatians 5:25: "Since this is the kind of life we have chosen, the life of the Spirit, let us make sure that we do not just hold it as *an idea in our heads or a sentiment in our hearts,* but work out its implications in every detail of our lives" (italics are mine). Mere ideas and changeable feelings do not themselves lead to action. Or as Lewis put in the mouth of Screwtape, his nephew Wormwood must "prevent his doing anything. As long as he does not convert it into action, it does not matter how much he thinks about this new repentance. Let the little brute wallow in it. Let him, if he has any bent that way, write a book about it . . . Let him do anything but act."[2]

All this sounds profoundly wise to me. Although I was struck by Lewis's rationality—as well as his imagination and emotion—when I first read him as a teenager, these certainly weren't the only elements of his work that sustained me. In fact, as I've learned from him over the past thirty years, and as I've seen him work in the lives of my congregations, his *wisdom* has played a major role. Because wisdom speaks to the center of our lives—biblically (not culturally) speaking to the heart—it leads to proper action. Being an eighteen-year-old, I needed a little sagacity, whether I felt like I needed it or not. Thirty years later Lewis's wisdom still speaks to me and to those I've nurtured, taught, and counseled as their pastor. It has helped me grasp the crisis inherent in the tyranny of feelings. This is a crisis no one I've met escapes—it is a crisis inherent in the human condition. Lewis speaks wisely, but he also sees the spiritual depth behind these crises.

THRILL, THEN WORK, THEN HAPPINESS

Lewis reminds us that most important activities in life begin with duty and end with true happiness.

He offers that all good things—like love—start with emotion but become better when we work hard, become less enthralled, and move past mere feelings to where real enjoyment can be found. This is the path of obedience. For example, Lewis wrote to Edith Gates in 1944, "we have no power to make ourselves love God. The only way is absolute obedience to Him, total surrender. He will give us 'feeling' if He pleases. But both when He does and when He does not, we shall gradually learn that *feeling* is not the important thing."[3] In other words, feelings do not constitute our love for God; they are the result of obeying God. It is our will—or the center of action, which the Bible calls "the heart" (not to be confused with our emotions)—that is central to God. God wants to move us to action, and that is why the heart matters to God.

So feelings come and go. But when Lewis looked at the central form of gift-love or charity, he described this as "an affair of the will."[4] God "will give us feelings of love as He pleases. We cannot create them for ourselves, and we must not demand them as a right."[5] In this regard, Lewis followed his great mentor, George MacDonald. When I did research in Wheaton College's Wade Collection, where Lewis's own books are kept and are wonderfully available to researchers, I poured over Lewis's own copy of George MacDonald's *Unspoken Sermons*, noting the places that Lewis underlined or set aside for a type of index he created at the back of the book. In his sermon "Suffered unto Death," MacDonald comments, "A man does not live by his feelings any more than by bread, but by the Truth, that is, the Word, the Will, the uttered Being of God."[6] Similarly, Lewis built his near disdain for feelings on the conviction of God's constancy. However we may feel, God's love for us is certainly not subject to the vicissitudes of feelings: "Though our feelings come and go, His love for us does not."[7] Lewis was marked by the insights of his mentor, including this in his anthology of MacDonald as well.[8]

Faith, like the rest of Christian behavior, is about the will as guided by reason. When Lewis addresses faith in *Mere Christianity*, he notes that faith and reason may be overcome by emotion and imagination, just as when the anesthesiologist puts a mask on our face, a childish panic may begin even if reason tells us that we have nothing to fear and that anesthetics are useful.[9] And so to be healed, we must submit to another. Incidentally, by noting Lewis's comments on faith, I realize that I have slipped into categories that span "crises specific to Christians" and "crises for all human beings." So I admit again that these categories aren't closed. The crisis of feeling is something we can't escape. Yet what astounds me about Lewis is that he can write on Christian belief in a way that employs common human wisdom.

He deals similarly with love. In his section on Christian marriage, he warns that the thrill of being in love cannot be permanent. Indeed, "People get from books the idea that if you have married the right person you may expect to go on 'being in love' for ever."[10] As a result, they will change spouses when they no longer feel love, thinking they have made a mistake. But thrills come and go: "The sort of thrill a boy has at the first idea of flying will not go on when he has joined the R.A.F. and is really learning to fly." And this is true throughout life, but we must remember it when we seek to love someone.

> What is more (and I can hardly find words to tell you how important I think this), it is just the people who are ready to submit to the loss of the thrill and settle down to the sober interest, who are then most likely to meet new thrills in some quite different direction. The man who has learned to fly and become a good pilot will suddenly discover music; the man who has settled down to live in the beauty spot will discover gardening.[11]

How I wish our attention-deficit culture would heed this insight. Here we meet that fundamental conviction that there is a progression: first thrill, then loss of thrill to be accompanied by hard work, then something really good—true happiness. I would also note, along the lines of experiences that all human beings share, that Lewis uses flying and gardening, not playing the church organ and studying the Bible, to exemplify his point. I'm fairly certain he didn't even have to make this decision. Naturally all of life falls under God's watchful eye and grace. This is "one little part of what Christ meant by saying that a thing will not really live unless it first dies." Let go of the thrill,

> Let the thrill go—let it die away—go on through that period of death into the quieter interest and happiness that follow— and you will find you are living in a world of new thrills all the time. . . . It is much better fun to learn to swim than to go on endlessly (and hopelessly) trying to get back the feeling you had when you first went paddling as a small boy.[12]

This second paragraph perhaps evokes his minster grandfather's voice. Lewis takes it home—he makes a conclusion for the practical difference this insight makes to his readers' lives. Most pertinent here: Lewis warns us that feelings come and go, but "the quieter interest and happiness that follow" come later. And we ought not to miss them . . . despite, I'm afraid, how many do miss them today if they live by the tyranny of feelings.

THE LAW OF UNDULATION

One reason we cannot live by feelings is that they constantly change. "Knowledge can last, principles can last, habits can last; but feelings come and go."[13] That is the nature of human life. Lewis believed that we live between various vicissitudes, which he dubbed "The Law of Undulation." This I take to be one of Lewis's signature insights. He put this into *The*

Screwtape Letters when the senior devil, Screwtape, is counseling his junior apprentice against taking too much credit for the dry periods in human beings when they are more susceptible to temptation. Humans are half spirit and half animal, thus "amphibians."

> As spirits they belong to the eternal world, but as animals they inhabit time. This means that while their spirit can be directed to an eternal object, their bodies, passions, and imaginations are in continual change, for to be in time means to change. Their nearest approach to constancy, therefore, is undulation . . . a series of troughs and peaks. . . . The dryness and dullness through which your patient is now going are not, as you fondly suppose, your workmanship; they are merely a natural phenomenon which will do us no good unless you make a good use of it.[14]

In this approach, Lewis is reminding us not to take our emotions—and more generally, our vicissitudes, our "undulations"—too seriously. In the low emotional times, Christians may be tempted to overrate our low points as signs of spiritual weakness. But he believed that even anxieties are not sins. "They are afflictions, not sins. Like all afflictions, they are, if we can so take them, our share in the Passion of Christ."[15] This is so because afflictions—or low points on the turbulent undulations of life—are simply in the nature of being human, not particular to Christian believers.

The reality of our undulations means that at other times, we simply need to take our afflictions less seriously. Consider what Lewis wrote on December 16, 1947, to his good friend Owen Barfield: "Things were never worse at The Kilns," and then he offers this postscript: "Of course the real trouble is within. All things wd. be bearable if I were delivered from this internal storm (*buffera infernal*) of self-pity, rage, envy, terror, horror and general bilge!"[16] Notice how this whole quote only makes sense with the light touch of "general bilge." He doesn't take all the other emotions, even grave ones like "rage" and "horror," too seriously. They are boundaried by "bilge," scummy water at the bottom of a ship. Sometimes our nasty moods constitute nothing more significant. Screwtape also counseled against overusing a particular temptation: "But don't try this too long, for fear you awake his sense of humor and proportion, in which case he will merely laugh at you and go to bed."[17] In fact, this is sound wisdom whether we admit there is a Screwtape behind all these undulations or whether it's simply a part of the quality of life as we experience it.

The opposite side of the ledger holds up for Lewis as well: we should not overrate the good times. He has a superb phrase he picked up from the seventeenth-century scientist and philosopher Blaise Pascal on the error of Stoicism: "thinking we can do always what we do sometimes."[18] In other words, when we feel strong and robust, it is enticing (at least it is for me) to think this is normal. Furthermore, we might be tempted to applaud our moments of energy and contentedness as if they were somehow signs of our spiritual state. But that conclusion is equally foolish. Once again, taking in common human experience and thrills as just that—and not some reward for walking victoriously with the Lord—would silence some fairly silly statements I've heard, whether from others or myself.

TO LOOK AT OR ALONG

But there is at least more reason we can't even truly grasp our own feelings—and it is central to Lewis's own discoveries that led him to happiness. In the end, we need not take our feelings overly seriously because they undulate, but also because we don't even know what our feelings truly are. Human introspection is, at some level, worthless. We are terrible at understanding ourselves.

In his little essay from 1945, "Meditation in a Toolshed,"[19] Lewis wrote that we can look *along* our feelings or we can look *at* them. In this profound, subtle, and compact piece, Lewis reflects on seeing a beam of light through a crack in the toolshed. He found he could look *at* the beam and the dust particles floating in it or *along* it to the outside, to the trees and to the sun, which is millions of miles away. Both were useful, but he could not do both at the same time. "Looking at" and "looking along" follows Alexander's distinction between *contemplation* and *enjoyment* that I mentioned in chapter 2. The problem is that once we contemplate in this sense we have destroyed the experience of simply enjoying. "[O]ne essential property of love, hate, fear, hope, or desire was attention to their object. . . . The enjoyment and the contemplation of our inner activities are incompatible."[20] Lewis's point is that neither is better than the other—although his contemporaries in the academic world privileged contemplation—but that we cannot do both simultaneously. As it relates to feeling, Lewis concluded that we cannot introspect and expect to grasp what we truly are. Once we look inside we lose the feelings we want to find.

Why do I bring that up here? Because Lewis firmly believed that we cannot trust our own feelings—as soon as we introspect, we change the feelings we are looking for. Furthermore, trying to endlessly discover the status of our feelings is a fool's errand; we only discover contentment when we look outside ourselves and obey what God wants. When we engage our will, then we can do the will of God.

EVALUATION

I close this chapter with a prediction: I think many readers will find my discussion of emotions odd. I honestly doubt many would consider these insights on the crisis of feelings as a signature achievement for Lewis. But I believe this discussion is incredibly important for us, because we live in an American culture overrun by the decision making of feelings.

I mentioned these insights to an older friend and more recent reader of Lewis. He had become despondent in light of his diminishing capacities. But he also found moments of elation. He wanted to know how this fit with his faith. I described how Lewis brought wisdom to these changes, these undulations. This offered some comfort, especially since he had arrived at faith late in life and perhaps hoped it would resolve times of despondency. I also recalled a short vignette from The Chronicles of Narnia, in which Lewis's brilliant mind weaves moments of psychological depth with poignant clarity. In *The Silver Chair*, one of his favorite characters, Jill, has just experienced tragedy. She's burdened by despair and starts to cry. She remains paralyzed. The narrator then offers this insight: "Crying is all right in its way while it lasts. But you have to stop sooner or later and then you still have to decide what to do."[21] Only when Jill figures out what to do can the story proceed. I've found that helpful advice when I'm tempted by self-pity. I've found Lewis a valuable mentor when I'm faced with the crisis of everyday feelings.

These insights become even more important when we truly suffer, and that is the topic of the next chapter.

Chapter 8

THE CRISIS OF SUFFERING

Nequaquam nobis divinitus esse paratam
Naturam rerum; tanta stat praedita culpa
(Had God designed the world, it would not
be a world so frail and faulty as we see.)

"De rerum natura 5.198–99" in *Surprised by Joy*

IN SOME WAYS, EVERYTHING I'M WRITING ABOUT CONNECTS TO THIS chapter because all involve the reality, threat, and crisis of suffering.

Ironically, C. S. Lewis never wanted to write about the contents of this chapter. Even in his quest for joy, Lewis had to concede, "I had been far more anxious to avoid suffering than to achieve delight."[1] In order to find the joy he wanted in life, he knew that he had to come to terms with suffering. In order to hold to faith in the Christian God—the God who is almighty and loving—he had to work out the crisis of suffering.

It is easiest to understand this in the context of a consideration of Lewis's early life. It's worth recalling the crisis nine-year-old "Jack" Lewis experienced when his beloved mother died of cancer and its implications for his faith. Though the young Jack was conventionally religious and a member of a Church of Ireland family, this trauma led him gradually to atheism. As he describes it, the path to unbelief began with prayer. He asked God for something very specific for his mother, which he wrote about in his autobiography, *Surprised by Joy*: "When her case was pronounced hopeless I remembered what I had been taught; that prayers offered in faith would be granted." Despite these prayers, on August 23, his mother died. "The thing hadn't worked, but I was used to things not working."[2] God—it appeared to this young, brilliant boy—was irrelevant to the crisis of suffering in life. If he was irrelevant to suffering, then God probably did not exist.

In less than one month after their mother's death, Lewis and his brother were sent away by their distraught father to a series of boarding schools. He arrived at the first of these, Wynyrd School, in Watford, Hertfordshire, in 1908. Lewis's brother had enrolled there three years previously. At Wynyrd School, Lewis was under the thumb of a sadistic headmaster who was shortly thereafter committed to a psychiatric hospital. (Due to a lack of students, Wynyrd was closed not long afterward.) Later in life, Lewis summarized his experience at these schools in a letter to a child who wrote asking Lewis about his Narnia tales: "I was at three schools (all boarding schools) of which two were very horrid. I never hated anything so much, not even the front line trenches in World War I. Indeed the story is far *too* horrid to tell anyone of your age."[3] That is quite a comparison and perhaps the reason that Lewis invested seven chapters in *Surprised by Joy* on describing his experiences in boarding school.

As noted above, Lewis enlisted and served in World War I, and he was wounded in April 1918. Jack's life after the war wasn't free from suffering and pain, to be sure, but the crises it caused were significantly abated by the time he took up Ashley Sampson's request to write a book on suffering in a series of popular theology called "Christian Challenge." Lewis had learned a great deal after his bombastic and heavy-handed *The Pilgrim's Regress*, which appeared seven years earlier in 1933.

The Problem of Pain is really his first apologetic work and demonstrates a lighter touch. There we see Lewis's honesty and humility. For example, he writes that he could not begin the book without writing a disclaimer: "If any man is safe from the danger of under-estimating this adversary [of serious pain], I am that man."[4]

It is no overstatement to conclude that Lewis re-experienced the trauma of his youth—the mother of two young boys dying of cancer—in 1956 when Joy Davidman was diagnosed with cancer. This time, however, there was a twist: Lewis was gradually falling in love with his new wife, Joy. He had respected her mind for years, and she devoured and cherished his writings. Having met one another four years earlier, in the intervening years, she had moved to Oxford with her boys, Douglas and David. Lewis and Joy got along famously (but not always with the approval of Lewis's male friends). Yet, because of Joy's Communist Party sympathies, the British government concluded that she needed to be sent back to the United States. In order to thwart what he believed to be an egregious error, Lewis married her in a civil ceremony, telling few of his friends, simply so that Joy would not be deported. Shortly after her civil wedding came the diagnosis of cancer. Realizing that theirs had blossomed into much more than a marriage of convenience, they were again married in a Christian ceremony while Joy lay in a hospital bed. After a prayer by Peter Bide, an Anglican priest known for his gifts of healing, she recovered briefly, and they enjoyed a honeymoon including a trip to Greece. (Lewis had only traveled between Ireland and Oxford to that point.) But within eighteen months she had succumbed to bone cancer. After her death, he wrote a piercingly honest reflection on this trauma, *A Grief Observed*, a book that echoes what he wrote twenty years earlier about not underestimating pain. In *A Grief Observed* Lewis expresses profound doubt about his faith in God in the face of emotional pain.

Lewis did not write these as detached speculations but as resolutions to his own traumas. Just to review a few of his major crises, they are his mother's death, the tyranny of boarding schools, the miseries of two world wars, and the death of Joy. Added to that are the difficulties of caring for his alcoholic brother and for Mrs. Moore, who slipped into dementia toward the end of her life. His insights into suffering are also resources for us that can help us through our own crises of faith and doubt. And to repeat: his reflections have been forged in the fires of crisis. That fact makes their wisdom durable.

For these reasons, all human beings face the crisis of pain and suffering. And since the vast majority of humankind believes in God—the figure is close to 90 percent in the United States—and we usually believe in a God who is good and powerful, we must ask how that God can exist when life hurts so much.

Put another way, the crisis of suffering could also represent a fifth apologetic for Lewis. For Lewis it seems to be the strongest argument against God. This is not a topic for purely intellectual speculation. It's also enormously personal. The questions I hear most often in my pastoral work circle around the problem of pain and suffering: the parents whose son has turned away from Christian faith, the young dad diagnosed with cancer, the wife whose husband left one day, leaving only a note on the dresser. I talked recently with a mother whose son was going through a difficult experience. Yet it was an experience that seemed to bring her son, after some years of meandering, back to God. She appreciated Lewis's insights into the purpose of pain because Lewis made sense of why God might use suffering to help her son come to know God. Lewis's words on suffering are tough but true. Or to use his own phrase, suffering presents a "severe mercy"—which is a phrase he used in writing to a student, Sheldon Vanauken, at the death of Vanauken's wife. In fact, Vanauken offers beautiful insight into Lewis's companionship in suffering:

C. S. Lewis was to be *the* friend in my loss and grief, the one
hand in mine as I walked through a dark and desolate night.
Other friends gave me love, and it was a fire to warm me. But
Lewis was the friend I needed, the friend who would go with me
down to the bedrock of meaning . . . he gave me not only love
but wisdom and understanding and, when necessary, severity.[5]

Vanauken's words could also summarize Lewis's companionship for his readers. He offers not only wisdom and understanding but also severity. This combination brings me to his
approach to suffering, or as he phrases it, "the problem of
pain." Lewis sought not primarily a speculative response but
a soul-shaping or spiritual one. The answer to the problem of
pain depends to a large degree on how we pose the question.

What, then, is the problem of pain (also called the problem of evil)? Most often this is phrased as a *why* question: Why
is there pain and suffering in the world when a good and all-
powerful God exists? And this is an important question.
Although Lewis willingly takes up the question of why, he
emphasizes more vigorously the *how* question: How do we
respond to a world of suffering? This chapter seeks to respond
to a series of questions: How do I make sense of the massive evil
in the world and affirm that good can still exist? What do we do
when we suffer and try to simultaneously believe in a good and
powerful God? Is there any good to be found in a world of pain?
In Lewis's writing, *pain* means both the hurts, usually physical,
brought on by the world around us and the *suffering* or *affliction*
that comes with the psychological traumas that pain causes.[6]

TWO NECESSARY THINGS FIRST

In order to grasp Lewis's resolution to the problem of suffering, two preliminary notes are necessary, one on human
suffering and God's love and the second on human love and
suffering.

Frequently, the problem of evil is solved through the necessities of freedom. If human beings are given the freedom to choose God's love or not, they can say no; they can blaspheme or simply ignore God. If they are offered the possibility of caring for others, they can also choose to be cruel. It is similar with natural evil: the same fire that brings warmth can burn the innocent faun trapped in a forest fire. Both moral and human evil—and the pain caused—result from the misuse of freedom.

I think this defense has merit; otherwise I wouldn't have made it myself in *Creation and Last Things*.[7] Lewis also presents some of these arguments in his chapter "The Fall of Man" in *The Problem of Pain*.[8] And yet it has telling failings and therefore must be incomplete. For one thing, freedom cannot be solely defined as the ability to do anything, including evil. In fact, the biblical traditions tell us that true freedom is the capacity to do the right thing. To do evil is to chose bondage. For example, Jesus's words in John 8:31–32 are, "If ye continue in my word, then are ye my disciples indeed; And ye shall know the truth, and the truth shall make you free." And later (vv. 34–36), "Verily, verily, I say unto you, Whosoever committeth sin is the servant of sin. And the servant abideth not in the house for ever: but the Son abideth ever. If the Son therefore shall make you free, ye shall be free indeed." Moreover, as Lewis himself realized—probably most poignantly in his analysis of the fall—Adam's sin is not entirely comprehensible.[9] I would even assert that Adam's rebellion is *absurd*, by which I mean that we cannot fully understand why a perfect human being would rebel against the good God who created him. There is an unreasonableness at the heart of evil that we can never understand.

Therefore, the concept of freedom provides some insight into the problem of evil, but this is a minor theme. Primarily Lewis took another tack. He reminded his readers that God's love desires to make us better. It is our suffering that is intended to make us surrender more and more to God. In that sense, Lewis's response to human suffering is that God uses pain to develop us, thus there is a soul-shaping element in suffering. (Soul-making approaches to this issue can be found in the church father Irenaeus and more recently in John Hick.) Lewis writes that we must remember "that the soul is but a hollow which God fills. Its union with God is, almost by definition, a continual self-abandonment—an opening, an unveiling, a surrender, of itself."[10]

The first topic Lewis clarifies is the nature of divine love. Here is one of the key sections that—in order to understand the full import of his argument—needs to be cited at length: "When Christianity says that God loves man, it means that God *loves* man: not that He has some 'disinterested,' because really indifferent, concern for our welfare, but that, in awful and surprising truth, we are the objects of His love."[11] For God to love us implies that God wants to change us. We tend to think of love as being accepting and nonjudgmental, as essentially hands-off. Trading on the range of biblical images for God's relationship with us, Lewis argues that we don't really grasp what we have requested.

> You asked for a loving God: you have one. The great spirit you so lightly invoked, the "lord of terrible," is present: not a senile benevolence that drowsily wishes you to be happy in your own way, not the cold philanthropy of a conscientious magistrate, nor the care of a host who feels responsible for the comfort of his guests, but [here the biblical images begin] the consuming fire Himself, the Love that made the worlds, persistent as the artist's love for his work and despotic as man's love for a dog, provident and venerable as a father's love for a child, jealous, inexorable, exacting as love between the sexes.[12]

The classic question is bringing together two statements: that an all-powerful, truly good God exists and that human beings (and the rest of creation) suffer. Couldn't that God simply uni-laterally decide to remove suffering from the world? Isn't that the nature of love, to take away pain? The resolution of these dilemmas, Lewis offers, exists in a proper understanding of love.

The problem of reconciling human suffering with the exis-tence of a God who loves is only insoluble so long as we attach a trivial meaning to the word "love" and look on things as if man were at the center of them. Man is not the center. God does not exist for the sake of man. Man does not exist for his own sake. "Thou hast created all things, and for thy pleasure they are and were created" (Rev. 4:11). We were made not pri-marily that we may love God (though we were made for that too) but that God may love us, that we may become objects in which the divine love may rest "well pleased."[13]

Lewis will not dwell on the abstract question of why: Why does a good and powerful God allow for evil? Instead he looks at how God uses suffering for a *purpose*—to make us better. This, given that God is omnipotent, seems to suggest that God causes suffering. Lewis instead emphasizes that the cost of freedom is that the world has suffering. God does not create it, but he will use it for our good.

As I mentioned above, some call this a soul-shaping approach to evil. Austin Farrer, a friend of Lewis and distin-guished philosopher and Anglican priest, made an early criti-cism: that this form of responding to evil banks on a certain "moralism"—not petty moralism or legalism, but one that underlines how our souls find *moral* development. About Lewis, Farrer writes that when he "considered man in rela-tion to God he viewed him too narrowly as a moral will, and that relation too narrowly as a moral relation."[14] He con-cluded that Lewis played this card too often. Naturally Farrer has a point—all this pain cannot be simply about our moral development especially in light of a world full of *nonhuman* pain and suffering. It may even add to our pains to think that God is behind all the suffering we experience. Lewis similarly doesn't try to soften the blow by saying that God suffers with us. Although God is compassionate, it is not in this book that God comes alongside and shares in our pain; that concept would have to wait for *A Horse and His Boy* in a scene where Aslan, the lion and Christ figure, becomes a cat to offer comfort to the main character, Shasta.

With Farrer's contention still in mind, Lewis has more to convey than mere moralism and more to express than what's in *The Problem of Pain;* the best use of evil is to help us to grow into the image of Christ. As Michael Ward, coeditor of *The Cambridge Companion to C. S. Lewis*, notes, Lewis's most commonly cited verse was, "My God, my God, why hast thou forsaken me?"[15] The crucifixion cannot be neatly summarized as something moral—in fact, the travesty of justice that brought Jesus to the cross is profoundly immoral.[16] Only God could use the immorality of evil to develop our moral character . . . or, as I have phrased it, to shape our souls. Evil, in other words, is the way God can develop and transform us.

Secondly, suffering is essential to human love, at least in Lewis's definition. "Love," Lewis wrote, "is not an affectionate feeling, but a steady wish for the loved person's ultimate good as far as it can be obtained."[17] Lewis's definition of love opens us to suffering. And so another way to understand pain is that it is implied in the nature of love itself. When Lewis, thirty years later, reflected on the different Greek words for love in *The Four Loves*, he reminded us that the nature of loving someone is that it opens us up to pain, but that pain is worth the greater good of love. (This comes from the section on charity, or gift-love.) Lewis reminds us of both the importance and cost of love: if we want to love, we will have pain. This conclusion was formed by his loss early in life, and Lewis admits he would like to avoid it. "Of all arguments against love none makes so strong an appeal to my nature as 'Careful! This might lead you to suffering.'"[18]

But Lewis realizes that a soft, comfortable, pain-free life hardly corresponds to the biblical definition and demands of love.

> To my nature, my temperament, yes. Not to my conscience. When I respond to that appeal I seem to myself to be a thousand miles away from Christ. If I am sure of anything I am sure that His teaching was never meant to confirm my congenital preference for safe investments and limited liabilities. I doubt whether there is anything in me that pleases Him less. ... One must be outside the world of love, of all loves, before one thus calculates.[19]

Lewis is just getting going. Ever the rhetorician, he challenges the reader to play out the implications of this kind of safety. To navigate purely via safety is to move in an orbit away from God.

> To love at all is to be vulnerable. Love anything, and your heart will certainly be wrung and possibly be broken. If you want to make sure of keeping it intact, you must give your heart to no one, not even to an animal. Wrap it carefully round with hobbies and little luxuries; avoid all entanglements; lock it up safe in the casket or coffin of your selfishness. But in that casket—safe, dark, motionless, airless—it will change. It will not be broken; it will become unbreakable, impenetrable, irredeemable. The alternative to tragedy, or at least to the risk of tragedy, is damnation. The only place outside Heaven where you can be perfectly safe from all the dangers and perturbations of love is Hell.[20]

Since pain is part of loving and since God is love, God uses pain to help us grow. God helps us to grow because God loves us. Pain therefore has several purposes—and purpose answers a certain "why," the why of intention. "He who has a why can endure any how" (a saying some attribute to Friedrich Nietzsche but that I can't find in his writings). For that reason—that Lewis offers some purpose for suffering—his reflections can offer hope and insight. They are pastoral even more than they are purely philosophical.

So how does Lewis see God using suffering for the purpose of our growth in faith? Though others might categorize his work differently, I have found five key purposes in Lewis's writings.

FIVE KEY PURPOSES FOR SUFFERING

Suffering Can Lead Us to Cling to God

As I mentioned above, Lewis's favorite verse was Jesus's cry of dereliction, "My God, my God, why have you forsaken me?" When we are in moments of hurt sometimes God seems to have abandoned us. The promises of God's companionship can seem distant or even nonexistent. And here Lewis does not play the card that "God suffers with us" (which is a popular theological argument today). He faces the brutal reality of these moments; in them we experience abandonment. He says they are hellish. Nonetheless, when we turn to God in those moments—as Christ did—we realize a central purpose for suffering, and God deepens our relationship with him. (Worth noticing in this citation is the allusion to Jesus on the cross. This reflection is not mere monotheism, but soaked in the particular revelation in Christ.) According to Lewis, this turning to God in suffering remains so central to our growth that the devil shudders. As the senior tempter, Screwtape, writes to Wormwood,

> Our cause is never more in danger than when a human, no longer desiring, but still intending, to do our Enemy's will, looks round upon a universe from which every trace of Him seems to have vanished, and asks why he has been forsaken, and still obeys.[21]

Once again we turn to Lewis's insights on soul shaping—pain, for those who see it through, trains our wills to stay fixed on God. Or maybe I should say that suffering *can* train our wills, much like hill climbing trains bikers to race more effectively and strengthens them. They might find this painful training worthwhile. (They might also decide to stop training because biking isn't worth it to them.) Once we have learned that faith also involves training through suffering, we learn faithfulness in our relationship with God.

Suffering Is God's Megaphone to Rouse Us

True faith implies full surrender to God. Sometimes the only way to get us there is through suffering. This is a tough truth, but Lewis, at least, was willing to say that we are often asleep or deadened to God's voice. We can become complacent. So God uses pain in our lives to rouse us. (I have to concede that this sort of conclusion contrasts with much of contemporary "feel good" Christian writing. Therefore I trust it.) Lewis estimates that our desire for self-will is an intoxicating addiction: "The human spirit will not even try to surrender self-will as long as all seems to be well with it." And he knows that if we are satisfied with our lives we will take whatever gift comes our way—whether food, wealth, sex, or good fortune—and forget the giver. "But pain insists upon being attended to. God whispers to us in our pleasures, speaks to us in our conscience, but shouts in our pains: It is His megaphone to rouse a deaf world."[22]

Lewis is frank and admits that this megaphone may turn us to God. It might also turn us away: "No doubt Pain as God's megaphone is a terrible instrument; it may lead us to final and unrepented rebellion."[23] Pain is no guarantee; it may cause considerable growth in faith or its abandonment. I am thinking of the various pastoral conversations I've had where the disappointment with God turns the former believer away. One of the most poignant contemporary examples is the New

Testament scholar Bart Ehrman, who describes his own story of leaving the faith while he served as a pastor of Princeton Baptist Church. He simply could not come to terms with the existence of God and the reality of pain:

> I finally admitted defeat, came to realize that I could no longer believe in the God of my tradition, and acknowledged that I was an agnostic: I don't "know" if there is a God; but I think that if there is one, he certainly isn't the one proclaimed by the Judeo-Christian tradition, the one who is actively and powerfully involved in this world. And so I stopped going to church.[24]

Ehrman has created a bit of a cottage industry of writing books about his disappointment, and even anger, with God and his disdain for the mistakes in the Bible and the authors who penned them. He stands as a brilliant exponent of the way that God's megaphone can simply make some followers go deaf.

But not all do. And my encounters with people of faith demonstrate that right in the midst of suffering, many find God, that God's megaphone of pain grabs their attention and slows them down enough that they can find God. So often we rush on with life and give little heed to God, who is the source of life itself, and there is nothing like a physical injury or an emotional wound to bring the pace of life to a crawl.

The need to slow down is fundamental to our return to God. When I looked back over my life as I was writing *Say Yes to No* (on the importance of nos, as well as yeses, in finding happiness), I realized that I couldn't go forward simply by pressing on faster. Instead I needed to turn around and slow down. For me, this realization came with a small modicum of physical and psychological pain—it involved a wake-up call of potential stress-related health issues.[25] Once again the wisdom of Lewis: to frame the book properly, I began with this insight from Lewis,

We all want progress. But progress means getting nearer to the place where you want to be. And if you have taken a wrong turning, then to go forward does not get you any nearer. If you are on the wrong road, progress means doing an about-turn and walking back to the right road; and in that case the man who turns back soonest is the most progressive man.[26]

Progress is the result a decisive U-turn. Sometimes we need to slow down, turn around, and get on the right track. Sometimes suffering does just that.

Suffering Can Lead Us to Humility

Another way that God gets our attention through pain is that pain makes us humbled and less self-sufficient. No longer is everything going right because of our own efforts. And thus we come to a place where we can find contentment in God. The opposite of humility is pride, the self-sufficiency that says we don't need God. Lewis helps us understand why humility is important to God:

> We must not think Pride is something God forbids because He is offended at it, or that Humility is something He demands as due to his own dignity—as if God Himself was proud . . . *He wants you to know Him: wants to give you Himself.* And He and you are two things of such a kind that if you really get into any kind of touch with Him you will, in fact, be humble—delightfully humble, feeling the infinite relief of having for once got rid of all the silly nonsense about your own dignity which has made you restless and unhappy all your life.[27]

The reality of humility sounds like a pyrrhic victory to the skeptic: "If that's the remedy for human rebellion, then what kind of God is this?" The point is not this terrible remedy, but how much more pernicious our pride and self-centeredness are. When I go to the dermatologist and she deadens pre-cancerous spots on my skin by spraying liquid nitrogen, which—if it's not obvious—causes a stinging pain, I don't respond with, "What kind of sadistic doctor are you?" Instead I think, "Skin cancer is much worse. I'll go through this if I have to." Similarly, the recompense for pain is truly freeing self-forgetful humility. This only makes sense if God, and our relationship with that God, is truly for the greatest good.

Suffering Breaks Down Our Idea of God

One of the great and painful discoveries that Lewis makes in suffering is that God is the great iconoclast who breaks down our overly simplistic images. We would like to believe God wants our constant pleasure, what a friend of mine once called "a world of bubbles and kittens." As Lewis writes after the death of his wife, Joy:

> My idea of God is not a divine idea. It has to be shattered time after time. He shatters it Himself. He is the great iconoclast. Could we not almost say that this shattering is one of the marks of His presence? The Incarnation is the supreme example; it leaves all previous ideas of the Messiah in ruins. And most are "offended" by the iconoclasm; and blessed are those who are not.[28]

Suffering is never something that human beings look forward to. As Lewis phrased it succinctly in *The Problem of Pain*, "Pain hurts."[29] We do not naturally seek it. Nonetheless, the resources Lewis offers can give us some strength when we go through times of suffering and pain.

Suffering Can Lead Us to Hope

Suffering is a sign that this world is not ultimately satisfying, and it is why we hope for a new world. The new world is indeed a fulfillment of this world, which means there is continuity and discontinuity—continuity because we will understand the experiences, but discontinuity since the new world will not have the decay and death that is implicit in our experience. The final book of the Bible, Revelation, states that most clearly, by proclaiming that in the new heavens and new earth, "God shall wipe away all tears from their eyes; and there shall be no more death, neither sorrow, nor crying, neither shall there be any more pain: for the former things are passed away" (Rev. 21:4). For human happiness, we need to grasp that the world is fallen and flawed. Putting hope in this world is therefore bound to disappoint. Putting hope in the fulfillment of creation, for which Lewis employs "heaven" as shorthand, allows us to properly enjoy our current experience. "Aim at heaven and you will get earth 'thrown in.' Aim at earth and you get neither."[30]

Below is an excerpt that ranks as one of the finest in Lewis's writing, a blend of spiritual insight and philosophical-theological reflection that I find so overwhelming that some-times it's hard for me to keep reading past it. I find myself putting the book down and reflecting on the stunning mix-ture of wisdom, poignant emotion, and piercing insight that Lewis evokes. These are not abstruse reflections—they have been forged in the fires of experience. Here he describes what suffering points to. (Notice also how this conclusion emerges out of Lewis's quest for joy.)

> The Christian doctrine of suffering explains, I believe, a very curious fact about the world we live in. The settled happiness and security which we all desire, God withholds from us by the very nature of the world: but joy, pleasure, and merri-ment, He has scattered broadcast. We are never safe, but we have plenty of fun, and some ecstasy. It is not hard to see why. The security we crave would teach us to rest our hearts in this world and oppose an obstacle to our return to God: a few moments of happy love, a landscape, a symphony, a merry meeting with our friends, a bathe or a football match, have no such tendency. Our Father refreshes us on the jour-

ney with some pleasant inns, but will not encourage us to mistake them for home.[31]

As I described above, Lewis desired joy throughout his life, and he ultimately came to faith in God by realizing that this world is not our home and that joy can only be realized fully in heaven. This final reflection brings us to the fulfillment of the story of God's creation.

As I type this chapter, a good friend is going through a six-year bout with cancer and thus the rigorous hazing of chemotherapy. He wrote in a Facebook post, paraphrasing Lewis, "We shall be true persons when we have suffered ourselves to be fitted into our places. We are marble waiting to be shaped." His response? "Still being fitted, I suppose." Lewis's response to the question of "why evil?"—or better of "what use is evil?"—tells us that his soul shaping takes place now, and that is good and happens at the hand of a good God. Lewis also insists that we know that the fit will find its fulfillment in the final chapter according to Lewis's understanding of the suffering. It brings us to the final chapter of this book as well as the last word of the Bible.

Chapter 9

THE CRISIS OF DEATH

So far I have felt the normal feelings of a man of my age—like
an old tree that is losing all its leaves one by one:
this feels like an axe-blow near the roots.

Tolkien in a letter to his daughter, Priscilla, just after Lewis's death

BY HIS OWN ANALYSIS, THE PRIMARY MOTIVE IN THE STORY OF C. S.
Lewis is a quest for joy. And *Sehnsucht* led him ultimately to
his faith in Christ. The longing for joy was, in a sense, a crisis,
and it was one that Lewis could resolve. But the fact of death
forced Lewis to a crisis that no human can resolve through
earthly means. Death is the great laughter of the universe at
all human attainments. It is, by itself, the ultimate statement
of futility. As Shakespeare (whom Lewis loved) wrote through
the voice of Macbeth:

> Life's but a walking shadow, a poor player
> That struts and frets his hour upon the stage
> And then is heard no more: it is a tale
> Told by an idiot, full of sound and fury,
> Signifying nothing. (act V, scene V)

Death is something no one can avoid. Death in fact forced
Lewis to write a third autobiography of sorts, *A Grief Observed*,

a searing reflection on the death of Joy, his wife. Death also forced him to realize the answer to this crisis must lie outside ourselves in the promise of God. As the longing for joy led him to realize and to argue in his apologetics, our disappointment with this world leads us to seek something more, which can be fulfilled only by God's promise of heaven.

The fact of death has required me to step back and look at Lewis's life. To frame Lewis's life, I could consider the deaths of two significant women close to him: his mother in 1908 and his wife in 1960. In middle stands his long-term relationship with Janie Moore and her death in 1951. His mother provided him with an early sense of comfort and joy; her death revealed to him the terrors that stand around the borders of life. There indeed would be no "settled happiness."[1] The death of his wife, Joy, stirred a profound crisis for Lewis. We do not have the same record of distress over the death of Mrs. Moore, perhaps because her death released her from suffering and, to some degree, her tyranny of demands over Lewis.

Here I cannot avoid a comment on Lewis's views of women, which can present a significant problem for contemporary readers of Lewis. His early writing includes a dismissive attitude toward women, which partly mirrors early twentieth-century English society, where (for example) Oxford University was an almost entirely male bastion. One egregious example from *Mere Christianity* is his description of roles within marriage. However one views gender roles in the Bible, Lewis's chapter is based simply on convention, not on any theological argument or, for that matter, sound reasoning. "If there must be a head, why the man? Well, firstly is there any very serious wish that it should be the woman?"[2] This smells of rank prejudice; it hardly seems fitting to Lewis's thoughtfulness. Some argue that he rarely encountered women who were equals intellectually, but this cannot entirely excuse Lewis.

And yet, when he met Joy Davidman and eventually married her, he came to a different understanding of women—this one clearly held her own in "dialectics." One of the discoveries of reading Joy's copy of *The Problem of Pain* at the Wade Collection was her frank assessments of the book. In the margins on one page, she exclaims, "This is hardly Jack at his best." And yet earlier, she underlines the phrase "dreaming inner warmth" and comments: "This for such phrases I love him. What a perfect image of the secret self!"[3] For that reason—that in Joy, Lewis found an intellectual equal and soul mate as his wife—her death brought a profound crisis. Because she arrived late in Lewis's life (he was almost sixty), her passing brought a new understanding of, appropriately enough, joy. Correspondingly, after her death Lewis's cries of anguish are stunning: "Did you ever know, dear, how much you took away with you when you left?"[4]

Between those boundaries, Lewis faced several other significant experiences with death. We cannot overlook the fact that Lewis experienced death firsthand, and at a fairly young age, as a soldier in World War I. War is one colossal death event. He spoke about the war and "the horribly smashed men still moving like half-crushed beetles, the sitting or standing corpses."[5] His famous pact with Paddy Moore to take care of his mother was actualized when Paddy died. And he lived through the horrors of World War II. After all, Lewis sets The Chronicles of Narnia within the context of the bombing raids of London, which forced school children to move to places of refuge outside of London.

So death, in some way, confronted Lewis, just as it threatens us all. It is a crisis for all human beings not particular to atheists or believers. "Man that is born of a woman is of few days and full of trouble," as Job 14:1–2 soberly reminds us, "He cometh forth like a flower, and is cut down: he fleeth also as a shadow, and continueth not." One common assault on

Christian faith is that it is generated to solve the problem of death and annihilation. But this is certainly not true in Lewis's works and his own experiences. His resolution to the crisis of death emerged for him over time, as his faith grew. And as I noted earlier, Lewis concluded that God has implanted in us a desire and a hope for something beyond this life. That indicates that death—which marks our lives as boundaried—must have a resolution somewhere beyond this life. Joy leads to hope in heaven. Still, even if God implants in us the desire for fulfillment, Lewis was quite convinced that we cannot seek life beyond this earth *before* we seek God.

FAITH IN GOD FIRST

Lewis did not believe that religious faith solved the crisis of death. He was utterly convinced that faith in God must be our starting point. Put another way, Lewis himself did not believe in Christ because of a need to believe in life after death; he believed in life after death because of his faith. For a whole year he believed in God and tried "to obey Him before any belief in the future life was given."[6] This he discerned in the ancient Jews who—in great contrast to their neighbors the Egyptians—had no strong belief in an afterlife. It is, in fact, my experience as well.

Similarly Lewis expressed disdain for those who valued immortality above knowing God. Lewis notes—with some level of horror and scorn—the experience of knowing a church leader who simply valued the afterlife without any belief in God,

> an old, dirty, gabbling, tragic, Irish parson who had long since lost his faith but retained his living. By the time I met him his only interest was the search for evidence of "human survival"... [and] the ravenous desire for personal immortality co-existed in him with (apparently) a total indifference to all that could, on a sane view, make immortality desirable."[7]

Lewis then comes to two conclusions of note: "I was too young and hard to suspect that what secretly moved him was a thirst for the happiness which had been wholly denied him on earth"—a reworking of the argument from desire that I outlined earlier and that reappears in this chapter. Secondly, Lewis, in his early twenties at that time, concluded that immortality as a topic disgusted him, and he shut it out of his mind.[8] This statement helps us to understand his comments in *Reflections on the Psalms* about coming to faith without a desire for immortality. It is likely that this experience provided the context for his contention that faith in God needed to be first, before belief in immortality.

Notably Lewis's feelings about the relationship of belief in immortality and God also worked in reverse: to believe means that we desire heaven, or everlasting life with God. Therefore we become more committed to the afterlife. Consequently Lewis had some major musings on death many years after his conversion. Almost all his life, he did not feel "the horror of nonentity, of annihilation. . . . I felt it for the first time only in 1947. But that was after I had long been reconverted and thus began to know what life really is and what would have been lost by missing it."[9]

THE DEATH OF ANOTHER: A GRIEF OBSERVED

We resolve the crisis of death not by insisting on immortality but by believing in the immortal God who promises eternal life (or "heaven," in Lewis's terminology). Once we have tasted a relationship with this God, we hate the thought of losing it. But just as death meets us individually and we can contemplate our own nonexistence, we can also hit head-on the terrible reality of losing someone we love. As I highlighted above, the latter horror first hit Lewis when he was nine and his mother died, and it happened to him again at the end of life when Joy died. The death of others was much harder to contemplate than his own. Here again, as he discusses his wife's death, note Lewis's poignantly beautiful style that glimmers with surprise in the very first sentence: "No one ever told me that grief felt so like fear."[10]

Lewis realized that our experience with the death of someone we treasure initiates not a moment, but a *process* of grief: "I thought I could describe a *state*; make a map of sorrow. Sorrow, however, turns out to be not a state but a process."[11] As I mentioned above, his honesty, particularly his anger even at Joy, is striking. It demonstrates the depth of this crisis. Most of all, death of another can shake our belief in God. And in *A Grief Observed,* we see a new Lewis, a rawer style, one content not to answer the questions of faith but to let the most disturbing questions hang in the air. It is his honesty with God that remains the most arresting feature of this book: "Not that I am (I think) in much danger of ceasing to believe in God. The real danger is of coming to believe such dreadful things about Him."[12] It is his frankness about God that heals because we have all learned that expressing our grief is the passage to its healing. And ultimately there is a recovery of faith (though it is not exactly as it was before):

> When I lay these questions before God I get no answer. But a rather special sort of "No answer." It is not the locked door. It is more like a silent, certainly not uncompassionate, gaze. As though He shook His head not in refusal but waiving the question. Like, "Peace, child; you don't understand."[13]

Questions we once believed we could solve become less urgent.

The death of another—and the closer that person is, the more we feel it—shakes us to the core. But Lewis believed the crisis of death found its response in the Christian doctrine of hope for the life to come.

THE REALITY OF HEAVEN AND HELL

Probably as much as any writer, Lewis worked to make heaven a subject worthy of our reflection. Lewis in this passage seeks to describe heaven, our future life. Taking "heaven" (as I've already mentioned) to mean for Lewis the fulfillment of creation, Lewis reflects on the way heaven will similarly fulfill each person's life:

> The mold in which a key is made would be a strange thing, if you had never seen a key: and the key itself a strange thing if you had never seen a lock. Your soul has a curious shape because it is a hollow made to fit a particular swelling in the infinite contours of the divine substance, or a key to unlock one of the doors in the house with many mansions.[14]

Heaven is our real home, but this is also the place to make a brief comment on its opposite, hell. Since Lewis connected heaven with faith in God, hell is conversely moving away from God, who is the source of life. So Lewis was not a universalist. And this fact unsettled Joy. When I read through her copy of *The Problem of Pain*, Lewis responded to the assertion that all will be saved with, "If I say 'With their will,' my reason replies 'How if they *will not* give in?"[15] In the margin of her copy, Joy wrote, "I think they will in the end." Though many today would make that connection—that God's love, when experienced in fullness, is irresistible—Lewis did not. First of all, he didn't find it supported by Scripture. In a May 13, 1946, letter to Arthur Greeves, he wrote, "About Hell. All I have ever said is that the N.T. plainly implies the possibility of some being finally left in 'the outer darkness.'"[16] And secondly, Lewis believed that the will (as we've seen in the section on feelings) was essential to human identity. Lewis's argument in his long parable in *The Great Divorce* is that a will continually turned from God in this life will not easily be turned toward God in the next. All our choices, Lewis argues, add up to create creatures who are destined for heaven or who are ready to close the doors on God and choose hell. He writes in *Mere Christianity* that "all your life long you are slowly turning this central thing either into a heavenly creature or into a hellish creature."[17]

At some point, the decision against God becomes final. God must respect our will, the will to accept or to reject God. Hell is the refusal to accept the offer that God has given us. For this reason "the doors of hell are locked on the *inside*."[18] It is our resistance to God's love that throws us into the outer darkness.

Hell for Lewis is a place of shadows, a place never meant for human beings.[19] Exercising a glimmer of his immense skills as a scholar of literature, he analyzes what Jesus says in the Gospels about hell. Three principal images emerge: punishment (the "eternal punishment" of Matthew 25:46), destruction (Matthew 10:28: "fear him which is able to destroy both soul and body in hell"), and privation and banishment ("the outer darkness" where the slave who hid his talents in Matthew 25:30 is sent). Lewis concludes that we should not focus on descriptions of torture to the exclusion of destruction and privation. "To enter heaven is to become more human than you ever succeeded in being in earth; to enter hell is to be banished from humanity. What is cast (or casts itself) into hell is not a man: it is 'remains.'"[20] Notice here that what remains "casts itself"—a phrase reminiscent of his other that the gates of hell are "locked on the inside." Thus existence in hell (such as it is) remains a matter of choice. Lewis adds one final reflection: Jesus emphasizes conclusiveness, not duration, in these texts. "Consignment to the destroying fire is usually treated as the end of the story—not as the beginning of a new story."[21] For Lewis, heaven and hell are not equally balanced. For him, hell exists this side of annihilation while heaven is fulfillment and the expansion of any true definition of life.

If hell is a shadowy place that ends the story, what is truly real is heaven, even more real than the "shadow lands" of earth. (Of course, this is the title of the Hollywood movie on the life and marriage of Lewis and Davidman. It is also part of the title of the final chapter of *The Last Battle*: "Farewell to Shadowlands.") Here Lewis's love of Plato—and particularly the latter's sense that there is another world for which we all long and to which we are headed, the world of the forms—colors his understanding. The most sustained fictional treatment of the afterlife comes in his final installment of The Chronicles of Narnia, namely *The Last Battle*, when all the key protagonists are killed. They see a world that is like their Narnia, but as Lucy explains, "This is still Narnia, and, more real and more beautiful than the Narnia down below."[22] In case this sounds to the reader considerably like Plato's world of forms, Lord Digory explains it quite clearly: "It's all in Plato, all in Plato: bless me, what *do* they teach them at these schools!"[23] Now perhaps much of this is in Plato, whom Lewis considered to be one of those geniuses before Christ who truly grasped the reality of Christianity, but Lewis adds something new: the reality of heaven is that our experience will be richer and more real than what we have experienced on earth. And so going to heaven means continuity with our earthly experience coupled with ultimate fulfillment. However heaven is described, it is our intended destiny, and we are to live in light of it.

LIVING IN LIGHT OF HEAVEN

"Aim at heaven and you will get earth 'thrown in.' Aim at earth and you will get neither."[24] I repeat the phrase here in a different context: to take in the reality of heaven significantly changes our lives in the here and now. Lewis's vision of heaven was that there was fulfillment, but he could not be blamed for thinking that what we do today does not matter. In the Wade Collection I discovered an unpublished manuscript (MS-190) named (somewhat uncreatively), "Fragment about the Parable of the Unjust Steward." This fragment evokes a key conviction of Lewis: the difference it makes to live in light of heaven. Incidentally, this discovery was so exciting for me that my notes are a bit jumbled, and so I'll do my best to paraphrase what I found.

The Parable of the Unjust Steward from Luke 16:1–9 describes a steward, or manager, who uses his boss's money to win friends just before being fired. Lewis makes several comments on this passage. Here are the final two: he speaks of a summons during which the steward is fired, thus realizing his well-being is elsewhere. Spiritually, this is the soul's conversion. Secondly, there is the joke—or what I would call irony—typical to Lewis's concept of Judaism, in which the weak overcome the strong. He sees this pattern in the Jews plundering the goods of the stronger Egyptians or when the evil Persian leader Hanan hangs on the gallows at the end of Esther. In other words, we use the goods of the world for purposes the world would never foresee. As he retells this parable, Lewis implicitly describes how he reformulated his ambitions in light of heaven. He abandoned the hope for fame that he craved as a poet in his young adult years when he took on Christian faith. When it did arrive through apologetics and children's fiction, he didn't seem to care.

Lewis helped me understand earth *sub specie aeternitatis,* that is, in light of eternity. He also guided me to the reality of our future hope, which was critical for me as a college student entering the yuppie world—the world I was told to conquer. And here I trust the reader will allow me one more reflection on how Lewis's reflections on heaven profoundly affected me. While on a vacation to celebrate my college graduation, I can remember reading Lewis's insights about the afterlife from *Reflections on the Psalms,* and they knocked me off my metaphorical feet. In it he pointed out that human beings are not made for time, but instead for eternal life. I have always been a person that laments the passing of time—the friend I can no longer call because death has intervened, the diminishing eyes and muscles that are endemic to aging. Lewis offered me insight into this crisis that resolved my inherent grief over the passage of time.

Several years after first reading this passage—which combines a wistfulness at the passing of time with a vigorous affirmation of our future hope—I returned to it as a newly minted pastor when I had to preach my first Easter sermon. I sought to somehow make our hope for another, better life real and vital for the congregation, and I turned to Lewis to help me demonstrate how our recurrent human experiences resonate resurrection. Here's the passage I used:

> We are so little reconciled to time that we are even astonished at it. "How he's grown!" we exclaim, "How time flies!" as though the universal form of our experience were again and again a novelty. It is as strange as if a fish were repeatedly surprised at the wetness of water. And that would be strange indeed; unless of course the fish were destined to become, one day, a land animal.[25]

There is inside us that profound yearning for something transcendent that surpasses time particularly. We are made for fulfillment, for heaven. Lewis knew this and, by all accounts, lived it.

LEWIS'S FINAL DAYS

In the classical and medieval tradition—which Lewis, of course, treasured—a good life was defined by knowing one's death and thus dying well. *Memento mori,* which means "remember death" in Latin, were artistic depictions of mortality meant to serve as reminders that it was better not to die in one's sleep or die quickly—as many today long for—but to know we're dying and therefore to die prepared and peacefully. In this light, God did seem to prepare Lewis for his eventual passing. When he almost died in the summer of 1963, he expressed some regret that he was brought back. As he wrote to a fairly regular correspondent, Mary Willis Sherburne, who apparently was dying too:

> Pain is terrible, but surely you need not have fear as well? Can you not see death as the friend and deliverer? It means stripping off that body which is tormenting you: like taking off a hair-shirt or getting out of a dungeon. What is there to be afraid of?[26]

He did not cower before the thought of his own demise. Similarly, writing to his long-term friend Arthur Greeves on September 11, 1963, he found it

> rather a pity I did revive in July. I mean, having been glided so painlessly up to the Gate it seems hard to have it shut in one's face and know that the whole process must some day be gone thro' again, and perhaps far less pleasantly! Poor Lazarus! But God knows best.[27]

But this reprieve also allowed several final, precious weeks with his brother, Warnie. When Warnie wrote a memoir about his brother's life, his final lines express a pathos that pierces my heart as I read them. He remarked on the return to the happiness of their boyhood in the imaginary games they played in the "little end room," a place for Lewis's fruitful imagination as well:

> The wheel had come full circle: once again we were together in the little end room at home, shutting out from our talk the ever-present knowledge that the holidays were ending, that a new term fraught with unknown possibilities awaited us both. . . . We were recapturing the old schoolboy technique of extracting the last drop of juice from our holidays.[28]

But that was not to last. Just before his sixty-fifth birthday, the nibbed pen of C. S. Lewis would never dip into the inkwell and scratch out another of his insights. I find the words of his brother poignantly spare and profoundly moving as they relate Lewis's last day on earth:

> Friday, 22 November 1963, began much as other days: there was breakfast, then letters and the crossword puzzle. . . . Our

few words then [at four] were the last: at five-thirty I heard a crash and ran in, to find him lying unconscious at the foot of his bed. He ceased to breathe some three or four minutes later.[29]

Warren could only add, in his brief memoir, "nothing worse than this could ever happen to me in the future."[30] He too knew the sorrow of losing someone close. Indeed he could not bring himself to attend his beloved brother's funeral. Instead he numbed his pain with alcohol (as he had throughout his life) and had to survive another ten years without his beloved younger brother.

It's clear what Lewis believed about heaven and thus life after death. If he was right about what he wrote, his place is now secure. It is also certainly better. As he wrote so movingly in some of the final words from The Chronicles of Narnia:

All their life in this world and all their adventures in Narnia had only been the cover and the title page: now at last they were beginning Chapter One of the Great Story which no one on earth has read: which goes on for ever: in which every chapter is better than the one before.[31]

A FINAL THOUGHT ON ST. CLIVE

As I've written this book, I've found myself poring over others' words about Lewis, several of his biographies and remembrances by friends, and especially studying every work by Lewis that I could get my hands on (including some unpublished pieces). All the time I've pondered the depth of this man and particularly the reason his words still resonate to the crises of millions and have not stopped speaking fresh insights to me. Lewis remains, for me, a constant source of interest and even mystery. I found that I wanted to truly grasp, to definitively summarize, what he expressed. I wanted to know more about why I continue to be stunned by his insights and where I disagree with them.

There are three reasons for this: First of all, Lewis was the voice that woke me up to the possibility of God, of that something more beyond this material world. The amazing thing is that there are other voices that have led me to Christian faith, but it is Lewis's that keeps leading me back, "deeper and further in" (to borrow a phrase from *The Last Battle*). So I suppose that, in some way, I'm repaying a debt I feel I owe to him. Second, I sense that I learn better how to follow Christ when I read Lewis, who was a beer-drinking, pipe-smoking, and certainly imperfect human being—thus not a classic saint by any means. But maybe that's why he speaks to me. And not only me since I believe his readers are also improved in the process of grappling with the crises Lewis faced and resolved. Somehow making his readers better remains central to the moral formation that's characteristic of Lewis's writings. And yet that's not all. There's something numinous as well, a voice that calls me deeper. And it still does. Using his words, it's what Lewis read in George MacDonald when he tasted something "holy" in MacDonald's words.[32]

Finally, it strikes me that Lewis represents a superlative translator of Christian faith, and that inspires me. I want to translate these ancient truths so that they can resonate in our contemporary world. But how to do this? The earliest Christian writers—following Jesus himself—took great pains to be comprehensible, using street language and stories taken from everyday life. In their determination to speak clearly, they never left the scandalous demands of Jesus's message. Too many theologians speak in impenetrable language, hardly caring whether the public can understand them. Lewis changed that approach by stepping aside from the precise, though often distancing, language of academics. Instead he wrote in plain English. Lewis's legacy is that he believed the strange hardness of Gospel remains its greatest strength, and he dared to use language as clear as crystal that tapped his creative imagination. This still makes good sense. That is why he still speaks to millions, and as I mentioned above, that's why *Time* could quite recently name him today's "hottest theologian."

Even as I type these lines, artists are preparing a memorial to Lewis that will be placed in the famed Poets' Corner at Westminster Abbey on the fiftieth anniversary of his death. It is an honor he will share with the likes of many writers such as William Shakespeare, Jane Austen, T. S. Eliot, John Milton, and William Wordsworth. Yes, many millions have found inspiration in his voice and resolutions to their crises. For that reason, it is natural that Lewis has become a Christian cult figure. This represents another sort of immortality. And yet, as I read the words of the man himself, I think he would find this lamentable. That's one reason I've coined the term "St. Clive" (which, as I mentioned, I jokingly call him) or the Writer of the Fifth Gospel (another quip by some admiring, though not idolizing, friends)—to keep my perspective. Yes, he has been an important voice for me, and I suppose I wrote this book trying to figure out Clive Staples Lewis once and for all.

I have never enjoyed writing a book so much, and I'm a little sad that I have arrived at the end. To be honest, I don't feel that I still totally grasp him, and yet I also sense that he's worth the continual effort. His good friend J. R. R. Tolkien once commented about Lewis, "You'll never get to the bottom of him."[33] Maybe the best method is to simply accept that advice and enjoy the journey.

NOTES

Chapter 1: Introducing C. S. Lewis

1. *Webster's New Collegiate Dictionary* (Springfield, MA: 1977).

2. C. S. Lewis, *Surprised by Joy: The Shape of My Early Life* (New York: Harcourt, Brace, Jovanovich, 1955), 21, italics mine.

3. Ibid., 115.

4. Here I am following the revised chronology in McGrath, *C. S. Lewis: A Life* (Carol Stream: Tyndale, 2013), 131–51, especially 146, as well as Andrew Lazo, "Correcting the Chronology: Some Implications of 'Early Prose Joy,'" *Seven: An Anglo-American Literary Review* 29 (2012): 55–59.

5. *Surprised by Joy*, 228.

6. "Religion: Don v. Devil," *Time*, September 8, 1947, http://content.time.com/time/covers/0,16641,19470908,00.html.

7. Walter Hooper, ed., *The Collected Letters of C. S. Lewis. Volume II: Books, Broadcasts, and the War, 1931–1949* (New York: HarperSanFrancisco, 2006), 674.

8. A. N. Wilson, *C. S. Lewis: A Biography* (New York: Fawcett, 1990), 211–14.

9. George Sayer, *Jack: A Life of C. S. Lewis* (Wheaton, IL: Crossway, 1994).

10. Wilson, *C. S. Lewis: A Biography.*

11. McGrath, *C. S. Lewis—A Life.*

12. See C. S. Lewis and E. M. W. Tillyard, *The Personal Heresy: A Controversy* (Austin, TX: Concordia, 2008).

13. Sayer, *Jack: A Life of C. S. Lewis,* 219.

14. *Surprised by Joy,* 225.

15. Letter to his father, August 14, 1925, in *The Collected Letters of C. S. Lewis, Volume I: Family Letters, 1905–1931* (New York: Harper Collins, 2004), 648–49.

16. Douglas Gresham, *Jack's Life: The Life Story of C. S. Lewis* (Nashville: Broadman and Holman Books, 2005), 157.

17. E.g., in his inaugural lecture at Cambridge, "De Descriptione Temporum" in *They Asked for a Paper* (London: Geoffrey Bles, 1962), 20.

18. See the 2012 report from Pew Forum on Religion and Public Life, http://www.pewforum.org/2012/10/09/nones-on-the-rise.

19. Walter Hooper brought many of these papers together in *God in the Dock: Essays on Theology and Ethics* (Grand Rapids: Eerdmans, 1970), but see especially "The Founding of the Oxford Socratic Club," 126–28.

20. Lewis, "Is Theology Poetry?" in *They Asked for a Paper,* 154.

21. "Christian Apologetics," in *God in the Dock,* 101.

22. *Surprised by Joy,* 223.

23. Alastair Fowler, "C. S. Lewis: Supervisor," in *C. S. Lewis Remembered,* Harry Lee Poe and Rebecca Poe, eds. (Grand Rapids: Zondervan, 2006), 103.

24. C. S. Lewis, *The Screwtape Letters* (New York: MacMillan, 1961), 52.

25. Lewis, "Weight of Glory," in *They Asked for a Paper,* 205.

26. Francis S. Collins, *The Language of God: A Scientist Presents Evidence for Belief* (New York: Free Press, 2006).

Chapter 2: The Crisis of Materialism

1. C. S. Lewis, *Mere Christianity* (New York: MacMillan, 1962), 6.

2. David Van Biema, "Religion: Beyond the Wardrobe: How C. S. Lewis, the Beloved Creator of Narnia, Became the Hottest Theologian of 2005," *Time,* October 30, 2005.

3. James Como, *Branches to Heaven: The Genuises of C. S. Lewis* (Dallas: Spence Publishing Co., 2008), 151.

4. Earl Palmer, "C. S. Lewis: Twentieth-Century Apologist" (lecture, First Presbyterian Church, Berkeley, CA, November 25, 1984).

5. Chad Walsh, *C. S. Lewis: Apostle to the Skeptics* (Eugene, OR: Wipf & Stock, 2008).

6. C. S. Lewis, *Miracles: A Preliminary Study* (New York: MacMillan, 1960), 5.

7. Steven Pinker, interview by Steve Paulson, *Atoms & Eden: Conversations on Religion and Science* (New York: Oxford University Press USA, 2010), 239.

8. There are several resources to pursue the philosophical context of Lewis's thought, but a good one to begin with is Alister McGrath's *C. S. Lewis: A Life*, 31–54, and *Surprised by Joy* is also a good source—you'll see the key references in the notes to follow.

9. Jocelyn Gibb, ed., *Light on C. S. Lewis* (New York: Harcourt, Brace, Jovanovich, 1976), 41.

10. Walter Hooper, ed., *The Collected Letters of C. S. Lewis, Volume III: Narnia, Cambridge, and Joy, 1950–1963* (New York: HarperOne, 2007), 462.

11. Walter Hooper, ed., "De Descriptione Temporum," in *Selected Literary Essays* (Cambridge: Cambridge University, 1969), 13.

12. Cited in *Miracles,* 15.

13. Richard Dawkins, *River Out of Eden: A Darwinian View of Life* (London: Phoenix, 2004), 155.

14. It was read on November 7, 1944, and published in *The Socratic Digest* in 1945.

15. *The Screwtape Letters,* 4.

16. John Polkinghorne, interview by Krista Tippett, National Public Radio, "On Being with Krista Tippett," May 29, 2008, http://www.onbeing.org/program/quarks-and-creation/transcript/2421.

17. Hooper, *God in the Dock,* 38–39.

18. Ibid., 39.

19. "Is Theology Poetry?" in *The Weight of Glory and Other Addresses,* ed. Walter Hooper (New York: MacMillan, 1949), 78.

20. Ibid., 81.

21. C. S. Lewis, *Poetry and Prose in the Sixteenth Century,* The Oxford History of English Literature Series (Oxford: Clarenden, 2002), 13–14.

22. C. S. Lewis, *Poems* (New York: Harvest, 1964), 61.

23. "Is Theology Poetry?" 164–65.

24. Ibid., 165.

25. *Miracles,* 12.

26. *Letters III,* 34–35.

27. Wilson, *C. S. Lewis: A Biography,* 226.

28. Sayer, *Jack: A Life of C. S. Lewis*, 308.

29. You can start with Victor Reppert, *C. S. Lewis's Dangerous Idea* (Downers Grove, IL: InterVarsity Press Academic, 2003) and Ric Machuga, *In Defense of the Soul* (Grand Rapids: Brazos, 2002).

30. Michael Ward, *Planet Narnia: The Seven Heavens in the Imagination of C. S. Lewis* (Oxford, Oxford, 2010), 218–20.

31. John Beversluis, *C. S. Lewis and the Search for Rational Religion* (Grand Rapids: Wm. B. Eerdmans Press, 1985).

32. One prominent example is Daniel Dennett's *Consciousness Explained* (New York: Back Bay Books, 1992).

33. A. N. Wilson, "Religion of Hatred: Why We Should No Longer Be Cowed by the Chattering Classes Ruling Britain Who Sneer at Christianity," *MailOnline*, April 10, 2009, http://www.dailymail .co.uk/news/article-1169145/Religion-hatred-Why-longer-cowed -secular-zealots.html.

Chapter 3: The Crisis of Meaninglessness

1. *Surprised by Joy*, 17–18.

2. C. S. Lewis, *The Pilgrim's Regress: An Allegorical Apology for Christianity, Reason, and Romanticism* (Grand Rapids: Wm. B. Eerdmans Press, 1993), 204.

3. *Surprised by Joy*, 7.

4. Ibid.

5. Sayer, *Jack: A Life of C. S. Lewis*, 52.

6. "Is Theology Poetry?" 164.

7. Cited in Alistar E. McGrath, *The Intellectual World of C. S. Lewis* (West Sussex: Wiley-Blackwell, 2014), 107.

8. *Surprised by Joy*, 220.

9. Ibid., 238.

10. *Mere Christianity*, 120.

11. *The Screwtape Letters*, 101–2.

12. "The Weight of Glory," in *They Asked for a Paper*, 208.

13. Ibid., 206–7.

14. C. S. Lewis, *The Great Divorce: A Dream* (New York: MacMillan, 1946), 72–73.

15. *The Great Divorce*, 109.

16. Gibb, *Light on C. S. Lewis*, 37.

17. "Weight of Glory," 200.

18. December 29, 1958, letter to Mrs. Hook, *Letters III*, 1004.

19. *Miracles*, 109.

20. Ibid., 110.

21. Ibid.

22. John Calvin, *Institutes of the Christian Religion*, ed. John T. McNeil, trans. Ford Lewis Battles, Library of Christian Classics (Philadelphia: Westminster Press, 1960), 1.3.1.

23. Justin Barrett, *Cognitive Science, Religion, and Theology: From Human Minds to Divine Minds*, Templeton Science and Religion Series (West Conshohocken, PA: Templeton, 2011), 59.

24. Ibid., 71, and *Born Believers: The Science of Children's Religious Belief* (New York: Free Press, 2012). This feature of early childhood has been termed "promiscuous teleology" by the psychologist Deborah Kelemen (in Barrett, *Cognitive Science*, 70).

25. Harold Arlen, with lyrics by E. Y. Harburg, "Over the Rainbow" (EMI).

26. Blaise Pascal, *Pensées*, trans. A. J. Krailsheimer (New York: Penguin Books, 1995), 4.

27. *Mere Christianity*, 33.

Chapter 4: The Crisis of Anomie

1. C. S. Lewis, *The Problem of Pain* (New York: MacMillan, 1962), 38.

2. *Surprised by Joy*, 201.

3. Ibid., 226.

4. *The Problem of Pain*, 38.

5. Lewis also worked out this argument in detail in *The Abolition of Man* (New York: MacMillan, 1947).

6. *Mere Christianity*, 17.

7. Ibid., 20.

8. Charles W. Colson, "The Conversion of a Skeptic," in *Mere Christians: Inspiring Stories of Encounters with C. S. Lewis*, ed. Mary Anne Phemister and Andrew Lazo (Grand Rapids: Baker, 2009), 83.

9. Charles W. Colson, *Born Again* (Grand Rapids: Chosen Books, 2008).

10. Colson, "The Conversion of a Skeptic," 83.

11. *Mere Christianity*, 21.

12. *The Screwtape Letters*, 24.

13. *The Abolition of Man*, 29.

14. Ibid., 95–121.

15. See, for example, Michel Foucault, *Discipline and Punish: The Birth of the Prison*, trans. Alan Sheridan (New York: Vintage, 1979).

16. *Mere Christianity*, 24.

17. See David Sloan Wilson, *Darwin's Cathedral: Evolution, Religion, and the Nature of Society* (Chicago: University of Chicago Press), 2002.

18. Barrett, *Cognitive Science*, 86.

19. *Mere Christianity*, 22.

20. Ibid., 139–40.

21. Collins, *The Language of God*, 21–31.

22. *Mere Christianity*, 111.

Chapter 5: Jesus and the Crisis of Other Myths

1. *Letters I*, 234.

2. Cited in Walter Hooper, *C. S. Lewis: A Companion and Guide* (New York: HarperSanFrancisco, 1996), 65.

3. See "Second Meanings" in C. S. Lewis, *Reflections on the Psalms* (London: Geoffrey Bles, 1958), especially 106.

4. October 18, 1931, letter to Arthur Greeves, *Letters I*, 976–77.

5. Ibid., 977.

6. *Surprised by Joy*, 223–24; cf. *Jack: A Life of C. S. Lewis*, 222.

7. *Reflections on the Psalms*, 129.

8. *Surprised by Joy*, 235.

9. *The Problem of Pain*, 24.

10. *Mere Christianity*, 56.

11. *Miracles*, 109.

12. "What Are We to Make of Jesus Christ?" in *God in the Dock*, 156–60.

13. Ibid., 159.

14. *The Lion, the Witch, and the Wardrobe* (New York: Collier, 1950), 45.

15. *Mere Christianity*, 65.

16. February 18, 1940, *Letters II*, 351. He also writes to Warnie on 28 April 1940 about an article in *The Guardian* about Barth, "Dr Karl Barth and the War, A Letter to a French Pastor," *Letters II*, 404. Again, this is something about Barth, not by him.

17. October 13, 1958, letter to Corbin Scott Carnell, *Letters III*, 980.

18. George Hunsinger, *How to Read Karl Barth: The Shape of His Theology* (New York: Oxford University, 1991), 278–79.

19. November 8, 1952, *Letters III*, 245–46.

20. *The Last Battle*, book 7 in The Chronicles of Narnia (New York: Collier, 1956), 164–65.

21. Though I have learned a great deal from several scholars on the history of Jesus such as Jon Dominic Crossan and Marcus Borg,

N. T. Wright has done the most significant work. Among his voluminous writings one could begin with *Jesus and the Victory of God: Christian Origins* (Minneapolis: Fortress Press, 1997).

22. October 18, 1931, *Letters I*, 976.
23. *Mere Christianity*, 58–59.

Chapter 6: The Crisis of the Bible

1. *Mere Christianity*, 6.
2. The latter comment comes from John W. Robbins, "Did C. S. Lewis Go to Heaven?" *The Trinity Review* 226, November, December 2003, http://www.trinityfoundation.org/journal.php?id=103.
3. October 1, 1931, *Letters I*, 975.
4. *Reflections on the Psalms*, 113.
5. *The Problem of Pain*, 70–71.
6. October 5, 1955, letter to Wise, *Letters III*, 652. See also n. 284.
7. *Reflections on the Psalms*, 111–12.
8. November 8, 1952, letter to Mrs. Johnson, *Letters III*, 246.
9. Especially Barth's paragraph 19 in "The Word of God for the Church," *Church Dogmatics II/I: The Doctrine of God*, trans. G. W. Bromiley, T. F. Torrance; eds., T. H. L. Parker, W. B. Johnston, Harold Knight, J. L. M. Haire (Edinburgh: T & T Clark, 1957).
10. *Miracles*, 134, n. 1.
11. "Myth Became Fact," in *God in the Dock*, 66.
12. October 13, 1958, letter to Corbin Scott Carnell, *Letters III*, 980.
13. May 7, 1959, letter to Kilby, *Letters III*, 1046.
14. Walker Hooper, ed., *Christian Reflections* (Grand Rapids: Eerdmans, 1967).
15. Ibid., 152, n. 2.
16. *The Allegory of Love: A Study in Medieval Literature* (Oxford: Oxford University, 1936), 130.
17. *Reflections on the Psalms*, 112.
18. "The Strange New World of the Bible," in *The Word of God and the Word of Man*, trans. Douglas Horton (Gloucester: Peter Smith, 1978), 28–50.
19. These citations are in *The Screwtape Letters*, letter 23.
20. *The Screwtape Letters*, 125.
21. Ibid., 125.
22. J. B. Phillips, *Letters to Young Churches: A Translation of the New Testament Epistles, with an introduction by C. S. Lewis* (New York: MacMillan, 1953), vii–viii.
23. Ibid.

24. "Modern Theology and Biblical Criticism," in *Christian Reflections*, 163.

25. *Reflections on the Psalms*, 112.

26. Ibid., 110.

27. Jerry Root, "Introduction" in *The C. S. Lewis Bible* (New York: HarperOne, 2010), xviii.

28. *Reflections on the Psalms*, 119.

Chapter 7: The Crisis of Feeling

1. December 7, 1950, letter to Mary Van Deusen, *Letters III*, 69.

2. *The Screwtape Letters*, 67.

3. May 23, 1944, letter to Edith Gates, *Letters II*, 616.

4. *Mere Christianity*, 117.

5. Ibid., 117–18.

6. George MacDonald, *Unspoken Sermons* (London: Longmans, Green, and Co., 1893), 141–42.

7. *Mere Christianity*, 118.

8. C. S. Lewis, ed., *George MacDonald: An Anthology* (New York: Touchstone, 1996), 13.

9. *Mere Christianity*, 122.

10. Ibid., 100.

11. Ibid.

12. Ibid., 100–101.

13. Ibid., 99.

14. *The Screwtape Letters*, 37.

15. C. S. Lewis, *Letters to Malcolm: Chiefly on Prayer* (New York: Harcourt, Brace, Jovanovich, 1964), 41.

16. December 1947 letter, *Letters II*, 818.

17. *The Screwtape Letters*, 69–70.

18. *Letters to Malcolm*, 11.

19. "Meditation in a Toolshed," in *God in the Dock*, 212–15.

20. *Surprised by Joy*, 218.

21. *The Silver Chair*, Book 4 in The Chronicles of Narnia (New York: Collier, 1953), 15.

Chapter 8: The Crisis of Suffering

1. *Surprised by Joy*, 228.

2. Ibid., 24.

3. Alan Jacobs, *The Narnian: The Life and Imagination of C. S. Lewis* (New York: HarperOne, 2005), 20.

4. *The Problem of Pain*, 10.

5. Sheldon Vanauken, *A Severe Mercy* (New York: Bantam, 1977), 185.

6. *The Problem of Pain*, 90.

7. Gregory S. Cootsona, *Creation and Last Things: At the Intersection of Theology and Science* (Louisville, KY: Geneva, 2002), 64–66.

8. *The Problem of Pain*, 69–88.

9. Ibid., 79–86.

10. Ibid., 151.

11. Ibid., 46.

12. Ibid., 47.

13. Ibid., 48.

14. Gibb, *Light on Lewis*, 40.

15. Michael Ward, "On Suffering," in *The Cambridge Companion to C. S. Lewis*, ed. Robert MacSwain and Michael Ward (Cambridge: Cambridge University Press, 2010), 210.

16. Ward, "On Suffering," 209.

17. C. S. Lewis, "Answers to Questions on Christianity," in *God in the Dock*, 49.

18. C. S. Lewis, *The Four Loves* (New York: Harvest, 1971), 120.

19. Ibid.

20. Ibid., 121.

21. *The Screwtape Letters*, 47.

22. *The Problem of Pain*, 93.

23. Ibid., 95.

24. Bart Ehrman, *God's Problem: How the Bible Fails to Answer Our Most Important Question—Why We Suffer* (New York: HarperOne, 2008), 4.

25. Gregory S. Cootsona, *Say Yes to No: Creating the Best in Life, Work, and Love* (New York: Doubleday, 2009), ch. 1.

26. *Mere Christianity*, 36.

27. Ibid., 113–14, italics added.

28. *Grief Observed*, 78.

29. *The Problem of Pain*, 105.

30. *Mere Christianity*, 118.

31. *The Problem of Pain*, 115.

Chapter 9: The Crisis of Death

1. *Surprised by Joy*, 21.

2. *Mere Christianity*, 102.

3. In her copy, it was page 128.

4. *Grief Observed*, 48.

5. *Surprised by Joy*, 196.
6. *Reflections on the Psalms*, 42.
7. *Surprised by Joy*, 201–2.
8. Ibid., 202.
9. Ibid., 117.
10. *A Grief Observed*, 7.
11. Ibid., 47.
12. Ibid., 9–10.
13. Ibid., 55.
14. *The Problem of Pain*, 147–48.
15. Ibid., 119.
16. *Letters II*, 710.
17. *Mere Christianity*, 86.
18. *The Problem of Pain*, 127.
19. Ibid., 125.
20. Ibid., 125.
21. Ibid., 127.
22. *The Last Battle*, 180.
23. Ibid., 170.
24. *Mere Christianity*, 118.
25. *Reflections on the Psalms*, 138.
26. 17 June 1963, letter to Mary Willis Sherburne, *Letters III*, 1430.
27. Ibid., 1456.
28. *Letters of C. S. Lewis*, edited, with a memoir, by W. H. Lewis (New York: Harcourt Brace Jovanovich, 1966), 24–25.
29. Ibid., 25.
30. Ibid.
31. *The Last Battle*, 184.
32. *Surprised by Joy*, 181.
33. *Jack: A Life of C. S. Lewis*, xx.

BIBLIOGRAPHY

This is a selected list. I'm including only those texts that have entered directly into my writing in this book or that form the background to what I've written. Certainly there are many more both by and about Lewis, and perhaps they've entered unconsciously into my thought, but I didn't want to overburden this bibliography with an exhaustive list from an astonishingly prolific writer.

BOOKS BY C. S. LEWIS

I'm often asked, "Where's the best place to start with to understand Lewis?" Certainly his most famous work, and perhaps the most definitive, remains *Mere Christianity*. A quicker read—with chapters that are punchy and that can be easily digested before bed—*The Screwtape Letters* has immediate appeal. My personal favorites are *The Problem of Pain* and *Surprised by Joy*: the former because it has some of Lewis's most profound insights on the nature of God and the latter because of the directness of Lewis's search for joy and thus God (although I would recommend skipping the overwrought chapters on boarding school). As for his fiction, The Chronicles of Narnia are his best and are justifiably famous. Though every book is brilliant, *The Lion, the Witch, and the Wardrobe* would be the place to start. (I agree with Alan Jacobs that this actually begins the series, not *The Magician's Nephew.*) That and *The Last Battle* stand out as the finest and most satisfying of the series.

The Abolition of Man. New York: MacMillan, 1947.

The Allegory of Love: A Study in Medieval Literature. Oxford: Oxford University, 1936.

Christian Reflections. Edited by Walker Hooper. Grand Rapids: Eerdmans, 1967.

The Collected Letters of C. S. Lewis. 3 Volumes. Edited by Walter Hooper. New York: HarperSanFrancisco, 2004–2007.

The C. S. Lewis Bible. San Francisco: HarperOne, 2010.

The Discarded Image. Cambridge: Cambridge University, 1964.

The Four Loves. New York: Harvest, 1971.

George MacDonald: An Anthology. Edited with a preface by C. S. Lewis. New York: Touchstone, 1996.

God in the Dock. Edited by Walter Hooper. Grand Rapids: Eerdmans, 1970.

The Great Divorce. New York: MacMillan, 1946.

A Grief Observed. New York: Seabury, 1961.

The Last Battle. Book 7 in The Chronicles of Narnia. New York: Collier, 1956.

Letters of C. S. Lewis. Edited, with a memoir, by W. H. Lewis. New York: Harcourt, Brace, Jovanovich, 1966.

Letters to Malcolm: Chiefly on Prayer. New York: Harcourt, Brace, Jovanovich, 1964.

The Lion, the Witch, and the Wardrobe: A Story for Children. Book 1 in The Chronicles of Narnia. New York: Collier, 1950.

Mere Christianity. New York: MacMillian, 1960.

Miracles: A Preliminary Study. New York: MacMillan, 1960.

The Personal Heresy: A Controversy. With E. M. W. Tillyard. Edited by Joel D. Heck. Introduction by Bruce L. Edwards. Austin, TX: Concordia, 2008.

The Pilgrim's Regress: An Allegorical Apology for Christianity, Reason, and Romanticism. Grand Rapids: Eerdmans, 1992.

Poems. Edited by Walter Hooper. New York: Harvest, 1964.

Poetry and Prose in the Sixteenth Century. The Oxford History of English Literature, Volume 6. Oxford: Clarendon, 2002.

The Problem of Pain. New York: MacMillan, 1962.

Reflections on the Psalms. London: Geoffrey Bles, 1958.

Selected Literary Essays. Edited by Walter Hooper. Cambridge: Cambridge University, 1969.

The Screwtape Letters. New York: MacMillan, 1961.

Spirits in Bondage. Public Domain, 1919.

Surprised by Joy: The Shape of My Early Life. New York: Harcourt, Brace, Jovanovich, 1955.

They Asked for a Paper. London: Geoffrey Bles, 1962.

BOOKS OR ARTICLES ON C. S. LEWIS

George Sayer—first a pupil and later a good friend of Lewis—remains the classic biographer of Lewis. For massive erudition and theological sensitivity, Alister McGrath has written the gold standard in two companion volumes, although it reads a bit wooden and would have really benefited from one more round of editing for style. I found myself reading and rereading A. N. Wilson's biography—probably because Wilson's winsome style and his sensitivity to Lewis as a fellow man of literary acumen makes this beautiful literature. It is indeed exquisitely written, and it is more critical of Lewis. Though Wilson is not always entirely careful about facts, the portrait that emerges is compelling.

Beversluis, John. *C. S. Lewis and the Search for Rational Religion.* Grand Rapids: Eerdmans, 1985.

Bresland, Ronald W. *Travel with C. S. Lewis.* Leominster, MA: Day One Publications, 2006.

Christensen, Michael J. *C. S. Lewis on Scripture.* Nashville: Abingdon, 1979.

Como, James. *Branches to Heaven: The Geniuses of C. S. Lewis.* Dallas: Spence, 1998.

Duriez, Colin. *The C. S. Lewis Chronicles: The Indispensable Biography of the Creator of Narnia, Full of Little-Known Facts, Events, and Miscellany*. Foreword by Brian Sibley. New York: Bluebridge, 2005.

Gibb, Jocelyn, ed. *Light on C. S. Lewis*. New York: Harcourt, Brace, Jovanovich, 1976.

Gresham, Douglas. *Jack's Life: The Life Story of C. S. Lewis*. Foreword by Christopher Mitchell. Nashville: Broadman and Holman, 2005.

Hooper, Walter. *C. S. Lewis: Companion and Guide*. New York: HarperSanFrancisco, 1996.

Jacobs, Alan. *The Narnian: The Life and Imagination of C. S. Lewis*. San Francisco: HarperSanFrancisco, 2006.

Lazo, Andrew. "Correcting the Chronology: Some Implications of 'Early Prose Joy.'" *Seven: An Anglo-American Literary Review* 29 (2012): 51–62.

McGrath, Alister E. *C. S. Lewis: A Life*. Carol Stream, IL: Tyndale, 2013.

———. *The Intellectual World of C. S. Lewis*. West Sussex: Wiley-Blackwell, 2014.

MacSwain, Robert and Michael Ward, eds. *The Cambridge Companion to C. S. Lewis*. Cambridge: Cambridge, 2010.

Phemister, Mary Anne and Andrew Lazo. *Mere Christians: Inspiring Stories of Encounters with C. S. Lewis*. Grand Rapids: Baker, 2009.

Poe, Harry Lee and Rebecca Poe, eds. *C. S. Lewis Remembered*. Grand Rapids: Zondervan, 2006.

Reppert, Victor. *C. S. Lewis's Dangerous Idea*. Downers Grover, IL: InterVarsity, 2003.

Sayer, George. *Jack: A Life of C. S. Lewis*. Wheaton, IL: Crossway, 1994.

Van Biema, David. "Religion: Beyond the Wardrobe, How C. S. Lewis, the Beloved Creator of Narnia, Became the Hottest Theologian of 2005." *Time*, October 30, 2005.

Walsh, Chad. *C. S. Lewis: Apostle to the Skeptics*. Eugene, OR: Wipf & Stock, 2008.

Ward, Michael. *Planet Narnia: The Seven Heavens in the Imagination of C. S. Lewis*. Oxford: Oxford, 2010.

Williams, Rowan. *A Journey into the Heart of Narnia*. Oxford: Oxford University, 2012.

Wilson, A. N. *C. S. Lewis: A Biography*. New York: Fawcett Columbine, 1990.

———. "Religion of Hatred: Why We Should No Longer Be Cowed by the Chattering Classes Ruling Britain Who Sneer at Christianity." MailOnline, April 10, 2009.

ADDITIONAL WORKS CITED

Barrett, Justin. *Born Believers: The Science of Children's Religious Belief.* New York: Free Press, 2012.

———. *Cognitive Science, Religion, and Theology: From Human Minds to Divine Minds.* Templeton Science and Religion Series. West Conshohocken, PA: Templeton, 2011.

Barth, Karl. *Church Dogmatics* II/1: *The Doctrine of God.* Edited by G. W. Bromiley and T. F. Torrance. Translated by T. H. L. Parker, W. B. Johnston, Harold Knight, and J. L. M. Haire. Edinburgh: T & T Clark, 1957.

———. "The Strange New World of the Bible." *The Word of God and the Word of Man.* Translated with a foreword by Douglas Horton. Gloucester: Peter Smith, 1978.

Calvin, John. *The Institutes of the Christian Religion.* Edited by John T. McNeil. Translated by Ford Lewis Battles. 2 vols. Library of Christian Classics. Philadelphia: Westminster Press, 1960.

Collins, Francis. *The Language of God: A Scientist Presents Evidence for Belief.* New York: Free Press, 2006.

Colson, Chuck. *Born Again.* Grand Rapids: Chosen Books, 2008.

Cootsona, Gregory. *Creation and Last Things: At the Intersection of Theology and Science.* Louisville, KY: Geneva, 2002.

———. *Say Yes to No: Creating the Best in Life, Work, and Love.* New York: Doubleday, 2009.

Dennett, Daniel. *Consciousness Explained.* New York: Back Bay, 1992.

Ehrman, Bart. *God's Problem: How the Bible Fails to Answer Our Most Important Question—Why We Suffer.* San Francisco: HarperOne, 2008.

Foucault, Michel. *Discipline and Punish: The Birth of the Prison.* Translated by Alan Sheridan. New York: Vintage, 1979.

Hunsinger, George. *How to Read Karl Barth: The Shape of His Theology.* New York: Oxford University, 1991.

Machuga, Ric. *In Defense of the Soul: What It Means to Be Human.* Grand Rapids: Brazos, 2002.

Peters, Ted, ed. *Science and Theology: The New Consonance.* Boulder, CO: Westview, 1998.

Phillips, J. B. *Letters to Young Churches: A Translation of the New Testament Epistles.* With an introduction by C. S. Lewis. New York: MacMillan, 1953.

Polkinghorne, John. *Belief in God in an Age of Science.* New Haven, CT: Yale University, 2003.

Wilson, David Sloan. *Darwin's Cathedral: Evolution, Religion, and the Nature of Society.* Chicago: University of Chicago, 2002.

Wright, N. T. *Jesus and the Victory of God.* Minneapolis: Fortress, 1997.